MEMORY LANE

Steve Thornton

Chapter 01	Growing up in Kimberley Road. Moving house Cricket.
Chapter 02	Starting school. All things rural. Commercial TV Pets
Chapter 03	Grammar school, down brook, football. Starting work. Marriage.
Chapter 04	Our own home. Canada. Dad's death. Richard born. Taking up golf.
Chapter 05	Sean born. Body on the beach. Leaving RR, Sheila dies. Riverside FC. Ganley's. Sean graduates.
Chapter 06	Hammards. Snooker at Potters. Exit. Richard and Dawn. Richard and Sam. Hospital.
Chapter 07	Trent Lock golf. Retirement. Sean, Kathryn and Jim. School reunions. Magpie dies.
Chapter 08	Richard takes up writing. Erewash 2012. Carole's friends. Jim dies.
Chapter 09	I take up writing. New car. Hetty dies. Contact with Mike Ronan. Hospital.
Chapter 10	Meeting with Doug Smith. Ken dies. Cricket essay. Covid.
Chapter 11	Caterpillars. Hospital again. Tom dies. Plymouth.
Chapter 12	Covid jabs. Wildlife.
Chapter 13	Visit to the Vics. Wildlife. NHS. History Book.
Chapter 14	Mike makes contact. Getting rid of car. Queen. King.
Chapter 15	Miscellany.
Addenda	
Obituaries	

4

CHAPTER 1

Frances Elizabeth Dewey was born on June 22nd, 1885, in the tiny village of Knipton, Leicestershire. Following the premature death of her mother, Frances left school at the age of 10 in order to take over the role of housekeeper to her father, John Charles Dewey, and her four brothers Ackerman, Charles, Ernest and Harry Silverwood. I can well imagine that she worked long hours looking after that lot for little or no pay and it must have been a relief to her when the cavalry arrived in the shape of George William Thornton. He was a gamekeeper by profession who was born in the nearby village of Branston.

Romance blossomed between the pair and on October 26th, 1908, they were married in the nearest church, which was at Croxton Kerrial and over the course of the next 17 years, they brought five sons and two daughters into the world. The family home was in Shelford, where their first four children, Gordon (August 28th, 1909), Donald (February 27th, 1911), Lionel (July 5th, 1913) and Edgar (April 23rd, 1916), were born. When the Great War finally came to an end in 1918, George was discharged from the army after serving as a grenadier and the family moved to Cherry Orchard, Bestwood, where Stanley (April 8th, 1920) and Edna (January 4th, 1922) were born. They were soon on the move again, this time to Hopwell Cottages, Hopwell Hall, near Risley, where Marjorie was born (November 16th, 1925).

They were constantly on the move as a result of George's efforts to find work within his profession. It was in inexorable decline and as one position closed, he was obliged to move on to find another. His relentless search was finally over when his services as gamekeeper at Hopwell Hall were no longer required and the family were obliged to vacate their cottage, finally settling at Idridgehay House, 10, The Ridings, Ockbrook. George managed to find work at Barrons Nurseries and then at Rolls Royce, Mountsorrell but he was to suffer a terminal decline in his health following the discovery of a malignant tumour in his face. He died on September 27th, 1948, aged 64. I wasn't even 2 years old and have no visual memory of him whatsoever, or even the sound of his voice. I have no doubt that Dad would have introduced us when I was new-born – that's what Dads usually do, isn't it? I don't know whether I am alone in this respect but the first two years of my life seem to be beyond the limits of my memory span. Perhaps we don't acquire a memory function until our second birthday?

Edgar Thornton served in the RAF during World War II, mainly in the Middle East where it tends to be very hot and dusty. I don't know how much action he saw out there but he managed to survive it all and came home in one piece as Corporal Edgar Thornton. On January 15th, 1945, he married Lucy, widow of Walter Matchett, who had died unexpectedly in August, 1942, while serving in the Middle East as chauffeur and batman to a Brigadier. His death was recorded as being due to heatstroke and, because of the logistical problems at that time, he was buried in Basra.

I don't know how, when, or where Lucy and Edgar first met, but I'm sure that my sister Kathleen and I are both grateful that they did. As soon as they were married, Edgar assumed his rightful place with Lucy at 35, Kimberley Road, Borrowash, the home which she had shared with Walter and their three children, Sheila, Thomas and Kenneth, who were now 16, 15 and 11 years respectively. Edgar had replaced not only Walter but also Walter's eldest son Tom as head of the household and it seems that this new domestic situation did not meet with everyone's approval at the time. That's another story which I should like to hear more of from either of the two people who are still here to tell it but I don't hold out much hope of that after all these years. The marriage of Edgar and Lucy was to be blessed with two children, namely myself, Stephen David, born on October 19th, 1946, and my sister Kathleen Elizabeth, born on December 1st, 1950. Whether we were actually a blessing may be a matter of opinion and open to debate but, all the same, Lucy and Edgar would henceforth be known as our "Mum and Dad".

Like most kids, I was independently mobile from the age of about 3 and it was not unusual for me to be out in the street on my trike, or my scooter. I remember my "Mobo" scooter (with rear footbrake) and my "Gresham Flyer" trike (front caliper brake and rear luggage compartment) with great affection. Kimberley Road was a "no through road" and traffic was scarce and pretty well restricted to Buxton's coal lorry, the horse and dray of the Redhill's milkman and, sometimes, the Doctor's car. I think Roy

"Dod" Dewsbury at number 27 owned the only car in the Road and that never went far because he was always cleaning it. Nevertheless, it must have been a worry for the mums, wondering where the kids were and what they were up to, even when they knew. I have distinct and happy memories of those early days in Kimberley Road and one of the most vivid must be the time when, aged about 3 or 4, I apparently went AWOL. This was a story that Mum used to tell about me being missing before she realised that I hadn't been under her feet lately and that it was also unusually quiet.

Once the penny had dropped, panic ensued and the search began. It seems that I'd wandered down to the cricket field at the bottom of the Road and found my way into the storeroom. Next to the mower was a can containing some of the watery whitener and a brush which Dad used to mark the creases on the cricket pitch. I don't know who found me but by the time I was discovered, the familiar green livery of the Qualcast mower was a mucky white. I don't recall getting any thanks for my efforts and, at the end of the day, I was only gone for about an hour and neither the mower nor I had come to any real harm. When the dust eventually settled, I think most folks saw the funny side of it all. When using the cricket field as a short cut between the new estate and the village, as many did, you may well have come across Dad as he was mowing the wicket with a mucky-looking Qualcast. His gaze would usually be focussed on the mower because it was vital that he kept his lines straight and parallel. Some folks, quite understandably, may have been puzzled by that hint of a grin on his face and the smile in his eye – well now you know.

Between the last house (No 38) and the meadow, stretching between Kimberley Road and Elm Street, there was a rectangular-shaped area of ground where constantly-smouldering craters could be found. These were about 6 feet across and 5 feet deep and were used as incinerators for the disposal of garden waste from the allotments and nearby houses. Most houses on the even side of the road had access to the allotments but the main entrance was at the end of Ladysmith Road, next to the old Exservicemens' Club site, and still is. I got the impression that No 38 may have been owned by Percy Rodgers, one of the three village greengrocers, who grew vegetables for his shop on the allotment. The

Loftuses lived in the last house (47) on the longer, odd side of Kimberley Road and beyond that it came to a "dead end". In those days, it was a "no through road" and vehicular access to the meadow beyond the hedgerow was by way of a double gate.

Measuring about 150 metres square (5 acres, I think), this meadow was the ideal size for a cricket field and it was, more or less, the geographical bulls-eye of the village once the new estate was created. It was good quality turf and, once the tufts and scrub had been tamed, it was then mown and manicured regularly until eventually it made the perfect home for Borrowash Wesleyan Methodist Youth Club cricket team. Councillor Frank Smith, a well-known public figure in the community for many years, was instrumental in forming the Youth Club and the team, making use of the experience he had gained from his 20-year association with O&BCC between the Wars. The Youth Club team played friendly matches between 1950 and 1956, after which time they had to vacate the ground because the land had been sold off for redevelopment. With no suitable alternative site within the village, the team was forced to disband – a disappointing end.

I believe the meadow may have been part of the 40 acres which William Barron originally purchased when he moved from Elvaston Castle to Borrowash to start his nursery business in 1865. I'd like to think that he may well have loaned or even donated the meadow to the community as a recreational area at some stage but I couldn't find any evidence of this. The fact that the Youth Club played there for six seasons suggests to me that the square had been properly laid at some time, probably before the War. It is unlikely that a natural meadowland square would have stood up to the wear and tear of cricket and pre-war Barron's staff such as Dad would have been able to locate the original square and restore it for the YC games. The meadow was bordered to the north by an orchard, to the south and west by hedgerows and to the east by the tree-lined Ock Brook, babbling quietly by on the last mile of its journey to the River Derwent. These completely natural surroundings gave the ground character and definition and to me, the place was like a magnet.

As we lived only 50 metres from the gate it made good sense to appoint Dad, a Barrons-trained, all-round horticulturist, as groundsman. In addition to these duties, he occasionally stood as Club Umpire and was even called up to play if the team was shorthanded, though he was almost 40 years old by then! The back of a Red Cross ambulance served as a storeroom for a variety of tools and spare kit. Dad's passion for the game inevitably rubbed off on me and since those early days, the traditions and principles of the game have coursed through my veins. Almost as soon as I could stand up he was teaching me how to hold a bat, how to catch a ball and how to bowl "spinners" and I just couldn't get enough of it. I was never a player of any consequence myself but I was, and still am, "out there kicking every ball", as the saying goes. When it comes to sport, cricket has always been my first love and I'm always ready to listen to anyone who wants to talk sensibly and knowledgably about the game. I believe that it pays to play with, and try to learn from, those who are better at it than I am, whether it be cricket or anything else. That way, there's a chance that I might learn quicker, pick up good habits and hopefully improve.

I despair at the way in which smart-arsed administrators and low-life cheats seem to dominate today's game because between them, these people create far more problems than they ever solve. They most certainly do not appear to have the best interests of the game at heart and seem intent on exploiting it. They are taking far more out of the game than they ever put in, whilst dragging its reputation and traditions through the gutter in the process. The largely unjustified and bloated salary levels of players, administrators and staff, regardless of overblown ability or status, have gone through the roof in recent times. I suppose that's true of any sport and we have TV rights, advertising and sponsorship to thank for providing the windfall finance which funds the system. Televised live cricket is available but only if we pay extra for the privilege and today's salary levels, which are funded almost entirely by this unearned income, portray cricket as a lucrative career. It gives a false impression of financial well-being, whilst in reality the game is certainly not self-sufficient and cannot independently support the extravagant personnel levels involved in the modern game.

We should take a step back and put the emphasis on educating our youngsters in the etiquette, technique and art of the purist game. If it continues to play second fiddle to the slogger's paradise of the "whackit-and-run-money-go-round" that is limited overs cricket, which seems to be the trend, then our beloved game is destined for the graveyard. We should also revert to the old system of selection for Test matches because the current "closed shop" contract system restricts our options when it comes to picking the best team available, based on current form. Issues surrounding the payment of players' wages whilst they are on Test duty would obviously need to be redressed. Prospective Test players who are striving to impress selectors must become so disheartened when they are overlooked in favour of the ever-present dinosaurs who continue to dominate the Test team.

It is no surprise that many of the next generation of talented players desert the game and move on to alternative careers. Free-to-air live TV coverage should be restored as a matter of urgency in order to allow easier access for all. Those who are stupid and selfish enough to go on paying are not only delaying this reform, but are also fuelling the dodgy system and making a rod for everyone's back. The vicious circle of "pay-per-view" needs to be broken and there has to be radical change from top to bottom otherwise the goose which is already straining to lay the golden egg will be in mortal danger.

Any hopes that Dad may have had of me playing cricket for Borrowash, or Ockbrook, or anybody else, were dashed before I was 10 years old, mainly because of the demise of the Youth Club team. This would have been an ideal opportunity for young players to get involved in the game. The Kimberley Road redevelopment plans eventually became effective in about 1961 and involved the extension of the Road in a southerly direction for about 150 metres, to the point where it crossed the culverted Ock Brook. Beyond that point, it would continue in an easterly direction as Balmoral Road, which would include a row of 5 shops, Briar Close and Barrons Way, where a new pub would be built to replace the demolished "Foresters Arms". The new "Foresters" pub opened its doors in about 1963 but, sadly, some of the patrons were inclined towards conduct of a violent nature and this did its reputation no favours. In one incident involving a knife-wielding drinker, one man died and several others were wounded. The pub eventually closed its doors for good in the late 1990s and was subsequently demolished and replaced by residential housing. The plans to extend Kimberley Road had been common knowledge for a good while but it was still a major setback for Borrowash cricket when they were finally implemented.

My all-too-brief career in representative cricket blossomed, peaked and died over a period of about 3 weeks during my third year at Grammar School, when I was selected to represent Soar in a couple of House matches. I wasn't much of a batsman but was in my element when it came to fielding, particularly in the slips, where concentration, a keen ear and eye, good reflexes and good hands are all useful assets. I managed to deceive a few with my "slow and bouncy" spinners, none more so than those who fancied their chances at hitting me out of sight. Times change, things move on and the folks in Borrowash don't have a Team of their own anymore, except maybe via "virtual reality".

I have no doubt that if we were to stand in the middle of the new part of Kimberley Road on what was the old square and close our eyes for a few seconds, our other senses would instinctively become heightened. At first, we become aware of the smell of new-mown grass and linseed oil, followed by the sound of leather on willow and cries of "Howzat"? We all turn to look towards the Umpire – will it be the raised finger, or the declining shake of the head? All so familiar on this very spot during that bygone age when it used to be our meadow. There is no harm in reminiscing now and then, taking time to reflect on the things which are precious to us and the things which make us tick and maybe other things that might have been, but weren't. Always safe in the knowledge that when we open our eyes, we'll be back in the real world. By remarkable coincidence, my brother Ken lived at No 71 for a while and this plot is pretty much on the site of the old cricket square – unbelievable!

For the final 18 months of the period between the Youth Club vacating the land in 1956 and the development contractors arriving in 1961, our once-hallowed ground reverted to its former status as a meadow, providing accommodation for 5 ponies (Shaun, Rom, Jacko, Pixie and Dixie), a retired racehorse (Sunup) and Mary the donkey. The animals were owned by a certain Mrs Tunnicliffe, a well-spoken, flame-haired lady who, I believe, lived on Vincent Avenue in Spondon and may have had connections with the military in some capacity? The arrival of the ponies in the neighbourhood attracted quite a few youngsters, most of whom had a parent in tow, and it wasn't long before Mrs T had a burgeoning riding school on her hands. She would spend time with beginners who were keen to learn, not only to ride correctly and safely, but also about cleaning the tack and grooming the animals. There was a code of conduct which was mainly, though not wholly, common sense and it was strictly enforced in an effort to minimise mishaps and the risk of injury to riders, animals or bystanders. A hard hat and crop were deemed basic essentials and without them, riders weren't allowed to mount up. When mounting up, it was always from the nearside of the animal and with the aid of a "leg-up" from someone, rather than putting one's foot in the stirrup and trying to climb aboard.

A mini obstacle course was set up so that the more experienced riders could school and exercise the ponies over small jumps – this was good practice for those who wanted to enter the local gymkhanas. It was popular with the riders and a welcome diversion for the animals, providing them with entertainment, stimulation and exercise. Jacko was a powerhouse and a puissance specialist – he could clear 5 feet with ease but only two or three of the riders could handle him. Even Mary couldn't contain herself amidst all the excitement and just had to break her silence now and then, just to let everyone know that she was there! Shelter was provided in the shape of a 25-foot marquee which also served as the tack room, despite the absence of any locks!

This venture achieved such a lot in a very short time and the youngsters were learning something useful and rewarding which they would be able to enjoy for a lifetime. It was disappointing when they were forced to move on to pastures new at Moor End, Spondon when the developers arrived. I made two or three trips to see them in their new home but it just wasn't the same. I was never really tempted into the riding and the highlights for me were a couple of trips to the blacksmith's at Allenton and Little Eaton, which were the nearest. Without the luxury of a horsebox we had to walk the ponies there and back and that meant a lengthy trip which took a full day, but it was an education in itself just to watch those craftsmen at work. The important thing was the reassurance of knowing that the ponies' hooves, legs and general well-being were being cared for.

Domestic changes were afoot in the summer of 1951 as we upped sticks to a new council house at 17, Ashbrook Avenue, which was about a 5-minute walk away if we took the shortcut across the cricket field and over the brook and up the 1-in-5 slope on the other side. Between numbers 17 and 19, there was a jitty which allowed access between the Avenue and the pathway which led down to the brook and then across the "rec" to Deans Drive. It was a busy thoroughfare on most days but especially so when people were toing and froing to school. Ours was one of about 250 new, semi-detached Council houses which were built in the 10-year period after the war, creating six new avenues in the process and the whole project was known as the Priorway Estate. I believe the land on which it was built was originally owned by Priors Barn Farm, hence the name. The farmhouse was tucked away behind Conway Avenue but that area has since been redeveloped to become Priors Barn Close.

Except for the pavements (which I helped to lay when aged about 6 or 7), about half of the Priorway Estate was pretty well near completion and ready for occupation by 1951. Nana, Auntie Edna and Uncle Stan Brecknock moved from Idridgehay House to 16, Harrington Avenue and Auntie Marjorie and Uncle Geoff moved from his parents' home in Edward Street, Stapleford to 41, Priorway Avenue. Our three families were now within 150 yards of each other and this obviously made visiting much easier for us, especially 66-year-old Nana and little 6-year-old me.

I was soon visiting Nana at least a couple of times a week as we made up for the belated start to our relationship and the more time I spent with her, the more I began to appreciate her ready wit and quiet manner. She had a way of catching your eye before she spoke to you so that she could be reasonably sure that you were paying attention. This meant that she didn't have to repeat things or raise her voice, both of which require extra energy and lung power which, for her, were limited in supply. There is no doubt that it was her humble demeanour which made the deepest and most enduring impression on me. I can well imagine that from an early age, like most who were born in the Victorian era, she had been brought up to know her place and that had obviously been a lesson well learnt.

By 1953/54, most of the new houses were occupied, some by folks like us who had simply moved from other parts of the village and others by folks who had moved into the village from other areas. That would almost certainly bring in extra business for the local tradesmen and one of those likely to benefit from the addition of new customers was the milkman. He delivered on behalf of the Redhill Dairy which was operated by the resident Gillett family at Church Farm in Ockbrook. With their own dairy herd and the facilities for milking, bottling and processing, the business was self-sufficient. Brothers Jim and Bill Burrows shared the duties in the yard and on the round, ably assisted by "BONNY", the grey dray horse. She had the patience of Job and was content to let Bill believe that, because she apparently paid little heed to his constant grumbling, he was in charge but she knew better. She weighed in at about a ton with hooves the size of buckets and she knew the routine of where to "wait" and when to "walk on" inside out. If, now and again, she decided to walk on when she should have been waiting, there wasn't a great deal that Bill could do about it. He could often be heard to growl the words, "Whoa, Bonny, damn your bloody eyes", usually to no avail. You'd think that might have been enough to remind him which of the pair of them was actually in charge.

A familiar sight in the village for as long as I could remember, they inevitably appeared on the streets of the new estate when I was about 5 years old. I soon became familiar with their route and knew where to find them at any particular time on the days when I wasn't at school. To start with, I just used to walk with them and watch – Bill seemed to appreciate that even my company had to be better than talking to himself. I quite enjoyed talking to Bonny, who always gave the impression she was listening but I seldom got any reply. Eventually, I got to ride in the box and help with deliveries here and there, just for an hour or so. I've no doubt that this would be considered highly irregular and probably illegal in these enlightened days, but I can't think that it did me any harm.

The intrepid pair covered the length and breadth of Borrowash and it was well after lunch on most days by the time they arrived back at the dairy but I was always long gone well before then. During my dalliance with the milkround, Bonny was retired and replaced by a diesel wagon named Morris Commercial. Before long, Morris was also retired and replaced by one of a fleet of new-fangled electric milk floats of the Derby Coop variety. Sadly, that signalled the end of the Redhill Dairy which, like most of the Independents, was not able to compete with the resources of the mighty Coop and was forced to abandon its delivery service. That, of course, meant the end of my career as a milkman, or at least I thought it did.

As a point of interest, the first Coop milkman to deliver on our street in the mid-1950s was known to us as Frank and he was involved in a fatal accident outside our house. The victim was a young girl who lived across the road who was waiting for Frank while he was taking his regular tea break next door at number 15. He eventually emerged but didn't notice her as he climbed into the float and as he pulled away, she was run over. Julie was the same age as me (about 8 at the time) and she died at the scene – we never saw Frank again. This was a tragic incident which affected the whole community, none more so than Julie's Dad Jimmy. He took to the drink for solace and was often to be seen lurching his way home from the pub. Some 10 years later, in early 1966 when I was working in No 4 Shop at Rolls Royce, who should come walking by one day but Frank. He had left his job at the Coop following the accident and had just started at RR as a labourer – what he did in between, I don't know. Small world?

There were other services which began to appear regularly on our streets, such as Len Bradbury. He used to turn out on Sunday mornings, together with his little pony "PEGGY", to collect our waste foodstuff. Peggy was hitched to a trap which contained a large cauldron and when it was full, Len would take it back to his smallholding where it would be hoisted onto heating apparatus, brought to the boil and then simmered for hours, eventually producing swill for his pigs. While this process was probably disgusting to look at, the aroma that wafted over the fence was actually quite pleasant. Troughs of pig pellets and bran were added to the menu and I imagine that it was quite appetising, if you were a pig, that is. Fed on grub like that, I imagine that the pigs looked quite appetising, if you were a human, that is. As Len collected our waste, Peggy would dump hers at various points along the route and the gardeners in the vicinity were soon on the scene with dustpan and bucket, even while it was still steaming.

Len lived on Nottingham Road, close to Shacklecross, and to the rear of his cottage was a narrow strip of land about 150 metres long which opened out into an orchard where the pigs roamed free to pick up any windfalls. There was a 6-foot wooden fence between the property and the adjacent twitchell, or "the Lantz" as it was known, which we couldn't see over, or through. When the new estate was built, the Lantz was reduced to a mere short cut between Nottingham Road and Charnwood Avenue. Once upon a time, it used to be the first section of a public footpath which went all the way to Ockbrook.

Directly across the road from Lens cottage at Shacklecross there was a paddock which was about 60 metres square and known locally as "Peggy's Field". As the name implies, Peggy happily spent her leisure hours there grazing and patrolling the perimeter fence cadging titbits from the many passers-by. Inevitably, Len and Peggy have long-since departed this life, as has Len's demolished cottage. Though Len and Peggy were irretrievably lost the cottage rose again like the Phoenix from the ashes in the shape of "Bradbury House", a new property built on the same site, but I don't know whether it is still in the family. Most of the land to the rear has been redeveloped to become Windsor Close, access to which is from Priorway Avenue. Peggy's Field now has about 10 bungalows on it, collectively known as Bradbury Close – a fitting tribute to a once-familiar pair.

Another sight which became familiar was that of William Radford's mobile greengrocery. His shop was at 3, Nottingham Road in the village, directly opposite Station Road, and Bill was one of three greengrocers with which the village was blessed. His main rival was Percy Rodgers who, I believe, may have been the owner of 38, Kimberley Road, just over the road from us. This house backed on to the allotments where he grew some of the produce for his shop, which was on Victoria Avenue, next to Coates the butchers. Bills other rival was Lakin's, whose shop was also on Victoria Avenue, on the corner of Elm Street and I think Bill stole a march on both of them with this master stroke.

He had acquired a single-decker coach (most likely a cast-off from Alan Parkin's Luxicoaches fleet), stripped the interior and kitted it out with shelving, scales, a counter and, of course, a till! He would do the rounds twice a week and I'll bet it was the best little earner he'd ever dreamt up and he even provided a two-wheeled barrow to help us get the heavier goods to our doors. A personal and complete service if ever there was one. As for the business rivalry between them, the demolition programme of the late 60s claimed Bill's shop, Percy's shop is now a Chinese takeaway and Lakin's is a carpet shop. I've no doubt that the Coop superstore in the village controls the monopoly on the greengrocery and most other things as well these days. I'll never understand why, when one business prospers at the expense of its competitors who cease trading, we call it progress?

There were several door-to-door callers who appeared regularly, including our popular Prudential Insurance man Ken Porter, the Kleeneze man Bill Tizzard and, of course, the Council Rentman, who was called quite a few names. Bill was the proprietor of a hardware shop on Station Road in Draycott and he would trudge to the door with his massive suitcase which must have been heavier than he was. Following the customary exchange of pleasantries, he would fling it open to reveal his wares - it was packed with every sort of household cleaning agent and implement you could imagine. Didn't I just love the fragrance of the polish and stuff – exquisite, like a lady's boudoir. That suitcase was surely the ultimate in the art of making best use of the available space, with a place for everything and everything in its place. Mum always used to buy something, even if it was only a couple of dusters and a tin of polish, just by way of thanking him for calling. I sometimes used to wonder how she could afford to buy dusters and stuff when she was forever telling me that I'd have to wait till Friday for my pocket-money because she'd just given her last quid to Dad for a "latch-lifter" at the Exservicemens' Club. Aren't Mums clever?

Dad always referred to his younger sister Marjorie as "Mag" and I thought that if it suited them, then it must be right and so it would do for me. Nana and my Aunties Mag and Edna used to make their way from their new homes on the estate to catch the No 8 Trent bus service into Derby on Saturday mornings. I think this ritual started because, following their moves to the new estate, it was now only a short walk to the main bus route into Derby. They would spend a couple of hours browsing in the posher shops and still be home by lunchtime. They had a shrewd eye for quality, whatever the commodity, and they always made a beeline for Birds the Confectioners for a selection of their delights, in spite of the length of the queue. Other targets on the itinerary included M&S, British Home Stores and Littlewoods.

Nana always had sweets in the cupboard for visitors and sweets in her handbag for when she was out and about, hence she became known endearingly as our "Tuttoo Nana". I used to visit her at least a couple of times a week to collect my "Blue Bird" chocolate caramels and an extra half-a-crown pocket money on a Tuesday (pension day), if I was lucky. I was also allowed to quaff the odd non-medicinal glass of Lucozade or Andrews Liver Salts, simply because they made a fizzing welcome change from pop. These visits went on 'til I was 13 or 14 because that half-a-crown would buy 10 fags or ½-an-ounce of "Golden Virginia" tobacco for "roll-ups" back then.

We benefitted greatly when Uncle Stan ("Brecky") invested in a new TV set at 16, Harrington, in preparation for the launch of commercial TV in about 1955. We were over the moon when he gifted us the old 14-inch Ferguson and it didn't really matter to us that our viewing was restricted to BBC 1. It was the only channel available at the time and those early TV sets weren't convertible. I seem to recall that, before the advent of commercial TV, broadcasting was restricted to evenings-only between 17:00 and 23:00. After that, our pictures were reduced to a single white dot in the middle of the screen until eventually that disappeared and all went black. Programmes were all good quality and included Muffin the Mule, Bill and Ben (both for kiddies), The Grove Family (TV's first soap), Bilko, Sooty, Perry Como and Charlie Drake, with a Francis Durbridge thriller serial thrown in for good measure. We had once-a-day news bulletins at 18:00, with the regular announcers McDonald Hobley, Sylvia Peters and Peter Haigh. This was our first TV and it wasn't everyone who had one in those days, so didn't we feel swanky!

Armchair euphoria aside, my most abiding memories of Nana are of the times when she ventured out to visit us, usually on Sunday evenings in the summer, weather permitting. For most, it was a short, 2-minute walk of 150 metres but it would take her a good 5 minutes but then again, she was never in any hurry over anything. Our back garden faced west and she would sit awhile in the early evening sunshine till she'd got her breath back and wiped the dewdrop from the end of her nose. Sometimes, the four of us and Kathleen in the pushchair, would take a steady walk to Ockbrook via what remained of the original public footpath from Borrowash to Ockbrook. As I've already mentioned, the first 200 metres of this path was "The Lantz" which ran alongside Bradbury's to Charnwood Avenue. The next section of the footpath between Charnwood Avenue and the end of Priorway Avenue disappeared when the new estate was built. The final 100 metres across the meadow from the end of Priorway Avenue to Cole Lane was still intact and remained part of our walk until it too disappeared in the late 1950s. This was following the development of Priorway Avenue, Sherwood Avenue, Depedale Avenue, Hawthorne Avenue and, of course, the sweeping wake of the A52. This stiled section of the path took us across the wildflower meadow which always looked a picture with its seasonal carpet of daisies, buttercups, campion, poppies, cowslips, clover, etc. (not necessarily in that order). It is only now, when so few of the meadows that we took for granted remain unspoiled, that some of us have come to realise, all too late, just how precious they were.

We would eventually arrive at the stile which gave us access to Cole Lane and then it was onward down Carrs Hill into Ockbrook village. I remember that there was a massive conker tree halfway down the hill and I used to scrump any that were overhanging the road. The safest way was to throw sticks to try to knock them off – that way you weren't climbing or trespassing. Our first port of call in the village was usually the Churchyard, mainly to pay our respects to Grandad George who, at the time, was the first member of our family to be laid to rest there, I believe. Inevitably, that list has grown over the years as he has since been joined at rest by Nana herself, Uncles Stan and Don Thornton and Aunties Edna, Dorothy, Mag and Phyllis. Mum and Dad were committed to the garden of rest in Plymouth, where they had latterly chosen to make their home. After a wander through the village, we would often call at the White Swan for pop and crisps before heading back home before darkness fell. By that time, there was often a chill in the air and I was glad of the jumper that Mum had thought to drape over the pushchair. Aren't mums clever?

CHAPTER 2

All this, of course, was prior to the advent of the A52 Borrowash Bypass in the late 1950s, when the excavators moved in to carve out the route. These monster scraping machines made short work of the wildflower meadows, footpaths and anything else that got in the way along the crow-flown 7-mile stretch between Bramcote Island and Spondon Lane End. Ockbrook and Borrowash were all but separated by the 40-yard-wide swathe of mud they created and although Cole Lane, Victoria Avenue and Borrowash Road were all navigable, it was a mucky business. The mud was superseded by a similarly-proportioned bed of hardcore topped with tarmac until the dual carriageway was eventually completed. The meadows which didn't become the A52 are now, for the most part, covered in houses and a walk to Ockbrook these days is via road only, with the aid of a footbridge over the A52 at Cole Lane. It is sited where the old footpath used to emerge from the meadow and was built to reconnect the severed footpaths on Cole Lane, thereby making the crossing of the A52 safer.

A footbridge was also installed at the Borrowash Road junction in Spondon and crossing the A52 by motor vehicle is not possible at either of these junctions following these changes and access to, and exit from, the A52 is by left-turn only. The changes were introduced following a series of incidents, some fatal, shortly after the road was officially opened in about 1958. The crossing of the A52 by motor vehicle is possible at Victoria Avenue, however, thanks to the flyover. Presumably, this option was necessary here because it is a main bus route to and from Derby which serves the villages of Borrowash, Ockbrook and Spondon. A time-consuming detour to Bostocks Lane and back or Spondon Lane End and back, depending on the route number, was probably not thought to be a viable or popular option, either by the Trent Motor Traction Company or their passengers.

The photo on the back cover shows me when I started at the Infants School, Derby Road, Borrowash, in September, 1951 and my first teacher was Mrs.Osborne. She always wore her grey hair in the style of a bun and she resembled everybody's Granny. She was a lovely, warm lady and ideally suited to comforting homesick little kids like me during those first few weeks. The ½-mile walk from Ashbrook Avenue to School took about 10 minutes and in those days, all parents walked the kids to school, often with a younger sibling in the pram – hardly anybody had a car. We used to make our way down the hill to the brook, over the stepping stones, across the rec to the rutted cinder track that led up to Deans Drive. At the top of Deans Drive, we turned left onto Victoria Avenue and from there it was another 250 metres to Derby Road, before turning right for a further 50 metres to arrive at the School gate.

On the odd occasion when the brook was in flood, we used the alternative route into the village via Nottingham Road. This problem was solved in 1953 when a footbridge was erected by Derbyshire County Council workmen (rather than sub-contractors) and it is as sturdy now as the day it was built. Whichever route we took to the school gate, Mum would always give me a little hug before I went through it, followed by a wave after. Before I disappeared out of sight to the playground at the back of the school, I would always pause to look for a second wave, though I knew that in those few seconds, she'd have disappeared. The School building is long-gone but part of the original wall between the school and Grandma Matchett's cottage next door is still intact to this day, I believe.

There was no pre-school playgroup or creche to prepare us for the shock of leaving home for the first time and I don't think that I ever got used to that – homesick is the word. Quite often at morning playtime, I would sneak round to Grandma Matchett's and she'd make me a sandwich of delicious home-made jam. The Staff knew where to find me whenever I went missing and it wasn't long before someone would come knocking to collect me. They eventually managed to get me house-trained and I progressed through Infants School, despite having to forfeit the sandwiches. I had plenty of help along the way from Miss Yarnold, Mrs Bramall and Mrs Talbot who were my teachers in years 2, 3, and 4 respectively and there was also a Mr Leeming in year 4 but I can't recall where he fitted in? Mrs Talbot lived at 28, Devonshire Avenue, next door to Bishell's, about 75 metres away from us. Somehow, I had managed to achieve standards which were always going to be difficult for me to maintain – prizes for high marks, top of the class and glowing reports. Was this the real me?

In September, 1956, I moved up from the Infants' to Ashbrook Junior School, or "Top School" as it was called, the entrance to which was, and still is, on Victoria Avenue, close to Deans Drive. Only a 5-minute walk from home now, but I had been making my own way to and from school since year 2 anyway. I was one month away from my 10th birthday when I started in Mr Jones' class for the first of my two years at the school. He was a very large Welshman with a proportionately large, rosy-red face to match and he was affectionately known to everyone as "Fatty" Jones. He lived at 37, Priorway Avenue, close to the Harrington Avenue junction and he used to walk to school with all the kids and mums, briefcase in hand. He did a lot of huffing and puffing but we soon came to realise that he was actually quite a friendly giant and not as fearsome as he looked.

I was looking forward to my birthday because a little bird had told me that Dad had bought me something special. The big day arrived and, as he handed me the small parcel, he said, "How old are you – 11?" I nervously corrected him and he just grunted, "Oh well, you'd better have it anyway". I removed the wrapping to reveal a presentation box containing a Timex "Hopalong Cassidy" wristwatch – my very first one. I don't remember what became of that watch but I dare say that I probably swapped it for a bag of conkers or marbles, or something equally worthless, as we did when we were kids. I remember the time when I swapped my cronky old bike for John Bishell's longbow but swapping Dad's present would have been an unforgivable thing to do. More fool me for not looking after it because those watches are now collectors' items with a market value of as much as £200!

To this day, I prefer to think that the confusion over my age was just Dad's idea of a joke. He had another joke which involved the use of props and these were in the form of a 1-inch curtain ring with two elastic bands tied to it. The free ends were attached to the looped ends of a bow-shaped, 6-inch length of 14-gauge copper wire. The ring was rotated, thus twisting the elastic bands and, when fully wound up, the primed equipment was then secreted 'twixt buttock and chair when taking one's place at the dinner table. By raising the appropriate buttock, the trapped ring could be controlled in such a way so as to allow it to unwind itself against one's seat, producing a sound not unlike the real thing. This was his "Fart-a-Phone" and the three of us fell for it hook, line and sinker.

Whilst Kath and I thought it mildly amusing that someone should break wind at the dinner table, Mum certainly did not and likened his manners to those of a pig. He was forgiven when he eventually revealed all amid fits of laughter, none louder than his.

The two years at the Top School were spent in preparation for the 11-Plus exam which lay ahead of us in the spring of 1958. Having negotiated the first year with Mr Jones, we then had the 6-week summer holiday before returning, with some trepidation, for the new term in September, 1957. I say "trepidation" because our final year was spent under the supervision of the diminutive, but formidable, Miss G.M.Johns (Gladys). Weighing in at about 7 stones and 5-feet-nothing tall, she had become affectionately known by successive generations as "Titch". Not only was this descriptive of her physique but it also distinguished her from her sister, the silver-haired Miss G.W.Johns (Winnie), the Headmistress. Some were fooled by the nickname but they quickly learned that her reputation as a disciplinarian was no myth and was well earned and she had no hesitation in dealing with anyone who crossed her lines.

I recall setting out for school on that first morning and meeting up with David Cluroe, who was visibly shivering when he asked me if I was scared. I think we all were, David. Yes, she ran a tight ship and now and again was as fearsome as she looked, but she was fair and as a teacher, was probably the best I ever came across. She was always willing to spend time helping anyone who was in need, whatever the subject, whatever the problem, whether academic or personal. All she expected in return for the sharing of her effort and expertise was that we should at least try to do the best that we were capable of. Even the clever dicks who thought they didn't need her help and had done enough were continually warned against resting on their laurels.

There is no doubt that her principles, her dedication and her enthusiasm were inspirational and I believe that the School and pupils benefitted enormously from the services of the Johns sisters over many years. In hindsight, I think that most of us who passed through the School during their regime look back on the experience as an education not to be missed. I was entrusted with special duties in that final year as milk and dinner money monitor, mainly because of my class record, I suppose. I remember letting my halo slip on one occasion, however, when I used the "bloody" word in the playground and was promptly reported to Miss Johns by Dickie Litchfield. I got three strokes of her ruler across the palm of my hand for my trouble and also some advice. Peering at me over her specs, she said, very quietly, "I'm surprised at you, Stephen. You should be more careful – that playground is full of tittle-tattlers". I had long suspected that there was a sense of humour lurking somewhere under that crusty exterior, though that experience wasn't funny. She was confident that if I continued to work as I had done, I should pass the 11-Plus with no problem and it was a relief to me that I didn't disappoint her. I know Mum and Dad were pleased, so much so that Dad's reward for my efforts was a spaceman's ray gun that fired caps! Suitably armed, with spare caps in pocket, I went on to continue my education at Long Eaton Grammar School in September, 1958, aged almost 12.

The leisure time in my early life seemed to be dominated by interests of a rural nature, initially with Dad's involvement with the YC cricket and then my dalliance with the Redhills milk round and Church Farm. By the time I was 8-years-old, the idea of growing up to become a train driver or an astronaut didn't really appeal to me. I wanted to be a farmer and, with this in mind, I thought it might be a good idea to visit my classmate John Shenton, whose parents owned a farm in Elvaston village. They had a Friesian dairy herd, which they milked on the premises, but no processing or bottling facilities and no delivery service. Instead, tankers would collect the milk and transport it to the bulk buyers for processing and delivery. The entrance to the farmyard was right on the main road, thus allowing instant access to the milking and storage area and plenty of room for manoeuvre for the tankers. If my timing was right, I was able to watch the herd pass through the automated milking stalls but it was the "Ferguson" tractor that caught my eye.

I had my first experience of "driving" when I was 5-years old when my brother Tom would sit me on his lap and let me steer Coates' three-wheeled Reliant van to the top of Deans Drive after taking his lunch break at Ashbrook Avenue. He would park it down by the brook and walk up the hill – this was quicker than going the long way around by road. This van was basically a 600cc motor bike with a box mounted on it and in comparison, the Fergie was positively deluxe. John had been brought up with this tractor and tear-arsing around on it was second nature to him. We took it into the nearest paddock and he showed me which bits did what and gave me some instruction and it wasn't long before this 8-year-old was kangarooing and stalling his way around the meadow! His Dad made no secret of the fact that he was keeping an eye on us from his position leaning on the gate whilst chuffing on his pipe. The legendary "Little Grey Fergie" was compact, neat, lightweight, versatile and popular with the ladies, apparently. Half-a-million of them were built in the 10 years following the War, mainly in Coventry, and a new one cost about £400 at that time. They were so popular that supply could never satisfy demand and some are still being used 70 years later.

By the time I was 10 and Kathleen had started school, Mum had taken a part-time cleaning job two mornings per week for a couple of hours, at the home of Mr and Mrs Henry Martin. They were a well-to-do couple in their 50s who lived in a large house on the eastern outskirts of Borrowash. When we leave the village on the B5010 and head towards Risley, it's the last house on the right before we reach Gypsy Lane. Mr Martin was a senior partner in the lace-making company known as Parry and Martin, or "Par Mar". Their business premises were at Draycott Mills, better known as "Jardine's factory", famous the world over for its clock tower. The Martins' son David, who was in his late twenties at the time, owned a smallholding which was to be found across the road from the main house at the end of a 150-metre-long cart track. He kept a few pigs and chickens and there was a barn where the bedding and feed was stored, along with his ageing tractor, a mighty "Fordson Major", and all its accessories.

Mum and Mrs Martin soon became good friends and probably spent as much time nattering as they did cleaning. Mum must have told her that I was keen on farming and Mrs Martin suggested that I go along and have a chat with David. I was a bit nervous about meeting such posh folks but Mrs Martin was a lovely lady, down to earth, with no airs and graces and I was made to feel at home from the word go. David appeared to be a scruff like me in his sloppy jumper, baggy corduroys and wellies, which he'd kicked off at the door, of course. Not the ordeal that I had expected and the outcome was that David invited me to call anytime and he would show me how to go about cleaning out the pigs and chickens and feeding them and changing the bedding. I recall hair-raising trips to Long Eaton along Sawley Road in his old van in the days when it was just a very narrow lane, before the advent of the M1 flyover and the reservoir. Flat out at 75mph and I'm sure that another 2mph would have been enough for us to take off! We made several stops at different places to pick up wood shavings, sawdust, corn, pig pellets, etc., which meant that the fully-laden return trip was usually a little more sedate.

It wasn't long before I graduated to tractor lessons and he seemed impressed that I had already broken the ice on the "Fergie" when only 8-years-old. Even I could see that the Fordson was a real workhorse and an altogether different animal. He took time to explain the controls to me and when all that had gone in one ear and out of the other, he fired her up and we did a circuit of the paddock, with me as the standing passenger. We then swapped places, with me taking over the driver's seat, and went around again. He then suggested that I go solo while he walked and with that, he jumped ship. I was only steering it at 5mph but to a nipper like me, this was a large, powerful machine and I found it needed all my concentration. It was a bit scary compared to the Fergie but I managed to do it without wrecking anything and he told me that I'd passed my test with flying colours and next time we would hitch up the plough and see how we go? The skill in ploughing, apparently, is in producing furrows which are straight but only when you've tried it do you appreciate just how skilful the ploughmen at the agricultural shows are. They make it look easy, whether the plough be tractor-drawn or horse-drawn.

In only a few short weeks, I became familiar with David's routine of running the place but it seemed to be nothing more than a hobby to him. Perhaps I was missing something but I couldn't see that he was actually producing anything in order to generate any income, even to cover his overheads. I came to the conclusion that either he'd had a win on the football pools or taken an early option on his parents' legacy. I think he must have sensed that I was at the end of my learning curve and he suggested that we pay a visit to the adjoining property, another small farm which was owned by the Atkinsons. The main entrance to the house and property was on Cole Lane but we took the shortcut across the meadow to the back door. It was a small, family concern which specialised in producing Channel Island milk from their small herd of

Jersey cows, with the automated milking, processing and bottling facilities all under the same roof. David left me in the capable hands of Mr Atkinson's son, who appeared to run the whole operation single-handedly, and he insisted that I should feel free to ask questions. I thoroughly enjoyed my visits and was impressed with how clean everything was, with machinery, paintwork and stainless steel equipment all pristine. A particularly fond memory is of the cute little calf that liked to suck your fingers while he was waiting for his mum in his calf-sized stall.

By the time I was 11 years old my farming ambitions suddenly and inexplicably seemed to evaporate, never to return – maybe it was the prospect of hard work and long hours. At some point, the Atkinsons' house was demolished and is no more – a new dwelling was built on the site. David Martin's smallholding is still shown on the A-Z street map, with the addition of a bungalow, built on raised foundations, halfway along the old cart track, which is now tarmacked. I had noticed this when passing in the car but I don't know whether the property is still operational, or inhabited, or by whom? I shall always be grateful to the Gilletts, the Shentons, the Martins and the Atkinsons for making me welcome, for their encouragement, and for allowing me to experience some of the more pleasant aspects of life on a farm. Thank you all.

In 1947, my Auntie Mag married Geoff Bowles, a Stapleford man. He was a mining engineer but, following the closure of his colliery in the early 50s, he subsequently joined Dad on the staff at Micafine. I took to visiting Geoff and Mag regularly after they moved to Priorway Avenue and they always made me feel welcome and wanted to know what I'd been up to. Geoff seemed OK but he had an unashamed hankering for socialising and rubbing shoulders with the local gentry. He seemed to think that frequenting their Saturday pheasant shoots and dinner-dance social events was a way of getting himself noticed. After 7 or 8 years of marriage, they still had no children and he sometimes took me with him on those mid-winter shooting trips, perhaps because he looked upon me as the son he'd never had? I remember the occasion when the two of us were invited to someone's home for liquid refreshment following the afternoon shoot. It turned out that our host was none other than the Director of Education for Derbyshire. Mixing with the bigwigs!

I was about 10 at that time and of an age when I didn't know much better and I quite enjoyed going with him, if only for the car ride. I remember that he had a pair of 12-bore shotguns which, to my untrained eye, were beautifully crafted pieces of engineering and it didn't seem right that they had been designed and built for the purpose of killing things and not simply for display. He had two gundogs – "JIGGER", a black retriever dog who was a real athlete and would probably have been capable of towing a Jumbo jet, and "BERRY", a golden retriever bitch who was unbelievably gentle and placid. The pair seemed to enjoy their trips out and they were incredibly responsive to Geoff's every word and gesture – it was an education to watch them working as a team. This pastime, however, was not really in my nature and to this day, I remain totally averse to the killing of unsuspecting, defenceless creatures in the name of sport or entertainment.

In the meantime, ITV had begun broadcasting in the London area in 1955, with programmes being networked through companies such as Granada, Anglia and ATV. I soon got an idea of the programmes on offer in the early evenings and would nip down to Auntie Mag's at the appropriate times. This additional network obviously meant a greater choice of programmes but the one fly in the ointment was the continual interruptions for advertisements. We have all since come to realise that the advertisers provide the funding and were, and still are, an essential part of the venture, hence the name "commercial TV". The first TV "game shows" appeared almost from day one and included Spot the Tune, Criss Cross Quiz, Take Your Pick and Double Your Money. The format for some of them was already established on radio and they were readily adaptable to suit the medium of TV. Many of the hosts of these shows went on to find fame and fortune in family entertainment and became household names – Hughie Green, Ken Platt, Bob Monkhouse, Ted Ray, Michael Miles, Eamonn Andrews, Jeremy Hawk, Marion Ryan and Des O'Connor were just a few.

I recall some of the early evening programmes such as The Buccaneers, Wagon Train, The Army Game, Robin Hood and William Tell, but I rationed my time as I didn't want to outstay the welcome. By now, Uncle Stan and Auntie Phyllis had moved from her parents' (Mr and Mrs Merriman) home at 24, Deans Drive, into one of the "Cornish" houses on the recently extended Conway Avenue. It was now a crescent which rejoined Priorway Avenue about 100 metres from Auntie Mag's. Only just around the corner, I would often call in at Auntie Phyllis' on my way home just to say hello in the hope that she might offer me a chocolate Brazil, or two. This would have been around 1959 when they were expecting their first child and it wasn't too long before they were on the move again to 167, Victoria Avenue. This was an older house which had a long back garden and that meant more room, not only for Uncle Stan's horticultural activities, but also for the new addition to the family.

I recall visits to The Sitwell cinema in Spondon with Uncle Geoff when I was about 11 or 12-years-old to see "Man of the West", and with Dad to see "Yangtse Incident", "The One That Got Away", and "Reach for the Sky". These films were all newly-released when we saw them and the latter 3 were based on true stories. The mid-50s was an exciting time for cinema-goers with the release of some real classics and some of the actors who featured in them went on to become screen idols. It was just as well that we made these trips when we did because The Sitwell closed its doors for the final time in 1958. It was around this time that Mum and Dad decided to extend our family with the addition of a dog and a cat. As far as I remember, these were the first pets we'd ever had in our house. Nurse Eames, our District Nurse, lived at 28, Deans Drive and she owned 3 corgis and all were involved in the Kennel Club breeding programme. It was through her that we acquired a long-haired Pembroke corgi puppy who we named "TONKA", though I'm not sure why, and he had a pedigree as long as your arm.

We'd hardly had time to get him home when Dad mentioned that the randy cat which belonged to his mate Frank Clifford had just produced another litter and did we want a kitten before he disposed of them? How could we refuse? About a month later, Dad came home carrying a shoebox which contained the cutest little ball of fluff we'd ever set eyes on. She was a tortoiseshell Persian and was barely old enough to be separated from her mother and so vulnerable, but here she was and we fell in love with her immediately. Dad said that she was the pick of the litter and he had no hesitation in laying claim to her and now we just needed to give her a name. Despite the conflict of gender, we settled for

"TAFFY", one of the male characters in "The Buccaneers" TV series, and that was that.

She all-too-quickly grew up to become the perfect domestic cat – she was never aggressive and seldom bared her claws when fussing and playing with us. I can see Dad now towing a screwed-up ball of paper around the garden on the end of a length of string while Taffy stalked it from the cover of the flower beds. She would eventually see her opportunity, her bum would waggle and she was on to her unsuspecting prey in a flash. Dad would give her a minute or two to "savour the kill" and when she was satisfied it was dead, she would sit up and begin to wash herself and that was the end of another game. When she was ready to go out for the night, she would sit by the door with her gaze fixed on the knob and there was no mistaking what she wanted. She'd disappear into the night and not be seen again until the next morning, when we would find her waiting to be let in at the same door, usually with a trophy on the doormat. And no, it wasn't a ball of paper this time! When at home with us she was always ready to show her affectionate side, whilst her lethal hunting skills remained outside until darkness descended once again, beckoning her to that private feline world.

During the late 1950s and early 1960s, Dad had taken the job of Groundsman at the new GIC Sportsground and on one particular Sunday morning he had gone to work at 06:00 to make final preparations for the afternoon cricket match. He was home by about 11:00 and he asked if I'd seen Taffy during the morning? He had been for a walk down the garden before going to work and found her lying in the cold frame and she didn't look very well. She was still there when I went to check and it was clear that we needed to see a Vet – but where, on a Sunday? The nearest phone was at Nanas and we managed to find a duty Vet in Sadler Gate, Derby. A gentleman who happened to be visiting Nana that morning very kindly offered to take us in his car. The Vet diagnosed problems with her heart and kidneys and said that she was very poorly and it might be best in the long run if we put her to sleep. This was all very sudden and seemed drastic but the thought that she may be suffering left us with little choice. As I cradled her in my arms I felt her go limp and I think she was gone before the Vet had even pulled the needle out.

Taffy was a very special cat who shared so much with us during her relatively short life and to lose her so suddenly in this way was devastating. She used to wait by my bedside most mornings so that as soon as I was up, she could jump in while it was still warm. Occasionally, she would jump the gun but I didn't mind because I knew that she must be ready for a snooze following her night-time activities and she made a lovely, purring, cosy pillow, just for 5 more minutes. To this day, she has a very special place in my heart. Tonka led a pampered life really and Dad took his turn when it came to grooming him but, in all honesty, he was rather spoiled. He was still going strong at about 10 years of age and made the move with Mum, Dad and Kathleen to Plymouth in 1969, where he died in 1974. Both Tonka and Taffy were special little people who were treasured members of our family and it was a privilege to have shared their lives and their trust.

CHAPTER 3

I started my first term at Long Eaton Grammar School in September, 1958, six weeks before my twelfth birthday. I had arrived with glowing reports from Borrowash Junior School and was assigned to form 1A, under the supervision of form master Mr Boardman, who was one of the maths teachers. Some may have had high hopes that I would continue my schooling in similar vein, myself and my parents included. It was a big step up and I wasn't sure what to expect when I started but, academically speaking, my five years at the School were disappointing. For reasons which I still cannot really explain, I never settled and from my second year I had my mind set on dropping out. I never quite came to terms with the idea that to stay ahead in schoolwork, you have to pay attention in the classroom and also make extra effort with homework. Basically, I did neither. When it came to a choice between spending my time doing homework or going "down brook", it was no contest and consequently, because I'd not done the work, I was forever in trouble. That meant, of course, that I was getting further and further behind and more and more discouraged.

I found myself in a vicious circle that just went from bad to worse to the extent that the mountain I now had to climb was almost certainly the reason that I lost interest in my schooling. I wanted to be anywhere but there and played truant sometimes in the hope that the School would kick me out but that just made matters worse. The School had other ideas and, in hindsight, I remain forever indebted to the Headmaster Mr Gray and his Staff for their perseverance and patience in helping me to sort myself out. Usually, we only get one bite at the cherry and Mum and Dad were not alone in being disappointed that I had not made the most of my talents and opportunities.

It was during my second year, however, I discovered that I was blessed with some limited ability on the football field and by the fifth year, I had represented the School at all levels from U13 to 1st XI. Between the ages of 12 and 14, I had worked for both James' and Coles', the two newsagents in Borrowash, as a paper boy. This came about mainly because of the deal I made with Mum to help me buy the Raleigh racing bike which I had seen in the window of Sims' cycle shop. She was prepared to sign the Hire Purchase Agreement provided that I made some contribution towards paying the instalments. Narrow racing wheels, drop handlebars and a Derailleur double-clanger with 10 gears and all for £30 – done! You may have noted that, despite my lapses, I did make it through to the fifth year and in June, 1963, sat 5 'O' Levels, managing just a single pass in English Language. I was one grade below a pass in Geography, Art, French and German. The hard part is having to live with the fact that I know I was capable of doing better than the records show.

One of the most positive and abiding legacies from Schooldays has to be that Carole and I started going out together during our final year. A certain Miss Kathy Kirby gracefully accepted the situation, since it was now plain that her efforts to lure me away weren't going to succeed. She faded from my life and went on to pursue a very successful career in the world of entertainment – sadly, Kathy died on May 20th, 2011, aged 72. Carole and I were married on June 8th, 1968, and are still here to tell the tale and so my time at Grammar School wasn't altogether a waste.

Despite firing blanks on the academic front, I think that I've turned out to be a reasonably decent sort of bloke, which has to be the most important thing. Mum and Dad came to terms with what was not to be and we all moved on but my conscience nags now and again and those all-too-familiar words "could have done better" still come back to haunt me. I suspect that I'm not alone in that regard. Whilst a fistful of diplomas may be something to crow about, there is no guarantee that they will provide a better lifestyle than the simple, fulfilling one which I have been lucky enough to enjoy. Failing to pass exams does not mean that you are a failure – it's what we're made of inside that matters above all else. At the end of the day, it has to be better to accept reality and get on with life rather than waste it daydreaming about what might have been.

During that final year at School, it was a real pleasure to have been a member of the musical ensemble known as "The Mustangs", together with schoolmates and vocalists/guitarists Derek Dickenson (rhythm), Doug Smith (lead) and Trevor Burton (bass). I became quite set on the idea of being the drummer because I could neither play a guitar nor sing, with a rating of "no-hoper" on both counts. My drumming was rated at only poor and barely bettered my singing and guitar-playing but the 3 guitars and the vocals managed to drown me out pretty well and we got by. It was a delight to work and play with the three of them and practice sessions were a welcome diversion. We were keen to learn and built up a repertoire of about 10 cover numbers but we never progressed to the point of performing in public.

I must confess, however, to making one gut-churning appearance at the Exservicemens' Club when Ferris Smith (Doug's Dad), who was a gifted pianist, invited me to accompany him during one of his regular Sunday evening slots. With some trepidation and no rehearsal, I eventually debuted alongside Ferris and, all things considered, it didn't go too badly. In hindsight, it was perhaps the best thing that could have happened to me because the experience served to convince me beyond any doubt that this "one-off" should remain just that. I am grateful to Ferris for his offer because, in accepting the challenge he laid down, I learnt that my place was in the auditorium rather than on the stage. I am neither a musician nor an entertainer but my experience with "The Mustangs" was unique and I wouldn't have missed it for the world.

Dad had always harboured hopes that one day I might turn out to be a cricketer of some sort but that was never seriously pursued. What bit of village green cricket I had played virtually came to an end when I started Grammar School simply because we were encouraged to play either football or rugby union. The School cricket team was virtually a 6th form closed shop. Surprisingly, I was selected to play football for the School U-13 XI and that coincided with the decision that we made to form a football team at the Youth Club in Borrowash. This would have been around 1959/60, by which time most of the Youth Club lads were playing for School at some level. The YC team joined the Derby Welfare League in 1961 and Dad used to turn up to watch our home games occasionally. It meant so much to me when I spotted him making his way down the hill to the touchline at Deans Drive on a Saturday afternoon.

I know how disappointed he must have been that I'd all but given up playing cricket and even if we'd won, congratulations were few and far between. The important thing was that, simply by turning up on the touchline, not only was he supporting the team but he was also supporting me in the choice I had made. Typically, he would say, "You ought to be playing for Derbyshire now instead of bringing half that bloody field home with you every weekend". I did play in two or three House matches for Soar during my third year at School, but that was pretty well the limit of my representative cricket. I'd by no means lost my love for the game but when it came to being actively involved, it was easier to join a football club than a cricket club.

Between the ages of 12 and 16, my social life centred around spending most evenings down on the rec, or "down brook", playing football or cards with the rest of the gang. For those in our ranks who were not inclined towards sport or gambling for pennies, there were alternative amusements in the form of swings, a slide and a roundabout. There were about 30 of us all together, lads and lasses, and I can well imagine that we may have looked quite a menacing bunch to anyone who didn't know us. In truth, I can't recall a single incident or occasion when our conduct, either as a group or as individuals, was ever questioned at any time. On the contrary, we did our fair share when it came to promoting the good name of Borrowash, in one way or another. The formation of our Youth Club team put Borrowash back on the footballing map after 5 years in exile and the all-important rebirth of Borrowash Victoria AFC in 1963 was a direct result of that. The legendary group "The Rapids" emerged from our midst and proved to be superb ambassadors for the village as they became one of the most popular and respected bands, not only in the Midlands but also nationally.

One or two of the local residents turned out to join in our footy kick-abouts and some came along to join the choir when they heard Maestro Beardsley strike up a chord and all were made welcome. We played football till we ran out of energy, we then played brag till we ran out of pennies or daylight and then we'd sing along to Beardsley's guitar till we ran out of puff, or the campfire ran out of flame. The music of Buddy Holly was more or less a religion to us, as it still is, and so there was no shortage of material for the choir to choose from. I take pride in the fact that 60-odd years later, I'm still able to croak along word for word on almost every track of this immortal music, such was its influence. I was 12-years-old and had barely begun to appreciate Buddy's talent when the news of his death in a plane crash on February 3rd, 1959, shocked the world. Musically, he was way ahead of his time and his contribution was certainly no passing fad and the circumstances surrounding his death make for a truly heartbreaking story. Many have tried to emulate Buddy but I doubt that his like will ever be seen again.

The names of the "Down Brook Gang", in no particular order – apologies to any that I may have missed.

Tony Beardsley	Tony Newton	Geraldine Williamson
Roger and Doug Smith	Rod Grounsell	Anne Tonge
Dave Whysall	Bob Shaw	Anne Coates
John Beniston	John Glenn	Val Burton
Richard Wheatley	Dave and Wilf Barsby	Dianne Salmon
Dave Wood	Gordon Illsley	Miriam Harrison
Bob and Jim Essex	John Nott	Jill Juffs
Graham Robson	Ray Wheatley	Carole Shaw
Derek Dickenson	John Church	
Paul Sutcliffe	Richard Litchfield	
Alan Hunt		

And so to bed as another day drew to a close after what was a typical evening for me during those 3 or 4 years and, whilst this lifestyle may appear to have been monotonous, no two evenings were ever the same. It was simple, it was free and there was never a dull moment when in the company of such a grand bunch of people. After Carole and I got together, my "down brook" life began to take a back seat as priorities changed. Life was taking me in a different direction and I eventually left Borrowash when we were married in 1968.

Our Youth Club football team played a series of friendlies during that first season and we did well enough to suggest that we should apply to join the League. As the newly-formed "Borrowash Youth Club FC", we started life at the bottom in Section E of the Derby Welfare League and our first League game was played at Deans Drive in September, 1961. We came up against another new team in the shape of Brunswick Rangers and the game finished at 5–5, a superb start for both teams and the spectators. Brunswick Rangers, Kilburn MW and Horsley Woodhouse MW were three teams who gave as good as they got and always gave us a run for our money but we won the majority of the other games and scored quite a few goals in the process.

I think we won promotion in that inaugural year and as the season progressed and our results were published, the folks in Borrowash were beginning to take notice of their new team. So much so that we had an offer from a gentleman by the name of Albert Anderton with regard to forming a Committee to look after team affairs, as opposed to appointing a Manager. Albert was well-known in the village but we weren't sure about his qualifications and did wonder if he would have made the offer had we been a team of losers? Allowing somebody else to shoulder the admin responsibilities seemed a sensible step to take and his offer was accepted. He wasted no time in appointing Oswald Whyman and Neville Hardy as fellow Committee Members, both of whom were Borrowash men through and through and familiar faces in the village. Almost immediately, the Committee proposed that we rename the Club "Borrowash Victoria AFC", thus adopting the traditional name of Borrowash football teams, the most recent of which disbanded in the mid-50s. The proposal was accepted and "The Vics" were reborn in time for the start of the 1963/64 season.

It was during 1964 that I played for the Exservicemens Club in the local darts league and this was just about the most nerve-racking sporting experience ever. When I stood on the oche to throw for a double to start, my raised throwing arm would tighten up and I was lucky to hit the board. I never mastered "the yips" and consequently my darts career was undistinguished and restricted to just a few matches, much to the relief of most, no doubt. It was perhaps a good thing because I never felt comfortable with the pub-orientated scene and Carole liked it even less. The decision to hang up my arrows was a no-brainer – you know when it makes sense. And yes, in those days we had to hit a double to start before our scores counted, akin to throwing a double six in ludo.

After changing the Club name, I enjoyed three or four seasons with the Vics, during which time we clambered our way up the League and managed to reach the Divisional Cup Final at the end of the 1963/64 season. This match was played on what was then a new pitch at the Celanese Social (Asterdale) Club Sports Complex in Spondon. Ironically, some 20 years later, this very same pitch became the Vics' new home in 1984 when the Deans Drive facilities were deemed unsuitable for higher grade football. The new ground soon became known as "The Bowl" because of its setting and improvements have been made over the years with the installation of on-site dressing rooms, social club facilities and also seating for about 500 in 2 covered stands. Floodlights were installed as a first priority and Brian Clough and his Nottingham Forest side were the guests for the inaugural match under the new lights in 1986.

Our Divisional Cup Final was an evening kick off, played on April 25th, 1964. We were up against Midland Mills, a Derby team who had already won the Section E Championship by 9 points and were going for "the double". I recall walking to the ground along Derby Road with my boots hung around my neck but, for the life of me, I can't remember who was with me? A few minutes before KO we gathered for Albert's team talk and as he handed me a shirt, he just said "Left wing, Steve" and there I stood with the No 11 shirt in my hands. I was pleased to be in the team, of course, but Albert knew that I was no left-winger and I was disappointed with that, to say the least, and I'm afraid I had a shitter! Derek Dickenson scored twice to drag us back into the game, which finished in a 2–2 draw and went to a replay at the Deaf and Dumb Ground on Ashbourne Road in Derby on May 1st. Predictably, I wasn't selected for this game and Ted Potter replaced Nobby Robson in goal. I was a mere spectator as we lost 1–0.

In the days following the replay, my disappointment festered into anger at being told to play so ridiculously out of position in a Cup Final and then dropped because I hadn't played well! I accept that we all make mistakes but, in my view, this tactical clanger cost us the match and I didn't appreciate being made the scapegoat. I am convinced that the team would have performed better had I played in my usual position at left-half and I am in no doubt that we would have won that Cup at the first attempt. At the time, Albert lived on Woodland Avenue about 200 metres away from us and, after waiting those few days for the dust to settle, I decided to pay him a visit. I let him know how I felt with both barrels and I can't recall that he and I had much to say to each other after that. He seemed to think that, because he was a close friend and relative of some of my family, respect for him ought to be automatic and that he knew best. Mum told me that he'd spoken to her about the incident and her reply to him was, "Stephen is sometimes easily led, but you won't drive him".

It was mainly because of this episode that I felt that the writing was on the wall for me at the Vics but there were also changes in the air at the Club and I decided that they weren't for me. Some over-ambitious body had big ideas about playing in a higher league but for me, being the consummate amateur that I am, the game was about enjoyment and sportsmanship and I thought that our village team was being usurped. Strangers were beginning to infiltrate the Club, one of whom was an ageing defender signed from Burton Albion who I thought was just a thug with a big gob. Another player arrived from Shepshed and he spent most of his time on the touchline nursing injuries of one sort or another. If this was progress, I wasn't impressed and I think my last game for the Vics was an away defeat at Derby Tech in March, 1966.

I look back on those days with great affection and feel privileged indeed to have worn that red-and-white-striped shirt with a black 6 on its back. There was a feeling of pride every time I pulled it on but for me, sadly, it all seemed to end prematurely on a bit of a sour note, what with one thing and another. Post-Vics, I went on to play a handful of games for Borrowash United and a few for Rolls Royce but my heart just wasn't in it anymore and by 1968, at the age of 22, my playing days were virtually over. No disrespect intended to either United or RR but it wasn't fair to them for me to continue, knowing that I couldn't give of my best because, deep down, there was only ever one Club that I wanted to play for.

I should like to take this opportunity to pay tribute to Eric Cockayne. I thought he was a good man and I'd like to think that a little bit of him may have rubbed off on all of us who knew him. He was extremely proud of all the players who helped him to build that super team at Borrowash United – his enthusiasm was boundless. I moved away from Borrowash in June, 1968, and it wasn't until 30 years later at the Borrowash Festival of Football that he and I were reunited. Ashbrook School hosted the event on Saturday, August 1st, 1998, and it featured a mini soccer tournament in the afternoon. I think this was designed to satisfy the cravings of the over-50s who still couldn't resist the temptation to try and kick a passing football! Later, we converged on the Nags Head for a social evening to round off a very special day.

During the afternoon, the non-playing spectators were gathered in groups on the touchline and as Eric came up to me, he gave me a bear hug and one of his toothless grins. He looked me straight in the eye and said, very quietly, "How's my star Vic?" Well, I don't know about that but that was typical of Eric – he had a way of making folks believe that they were better players than they actually were. Another 25 years have passed since that meeting and, wherever you are now Eric, I would like to say thank you for giving far more than you ever took.

As well as Uncle Stan and Auntie Phyllis moving to Victoria Avenue, there were other changes in the family domestic arrangements around that time. The most significant was probably Auntie Mag and Uncle Geoff deciding to go their separate ways in about 1958, leading to an annulment in 1960. I recall Uncle Geoff once taking me to a bungalow in Lime Grove, Chaddesden, which he was in the process of renovating. Not realising the significance of this at the time, it occurred to me subsequently that he probably moved in there when he and Mag split up.

That's probably the last memory I have of him and I don't recall seeing or hearing of him again until Mag mentioned that she had heard he'd died in about 2007. After the separation, she moved in with Nana, Edna and Stan at 16, Harrington, at least for a while until Stan and Edna moved to their new house at 86, Wilsthorpe Road, Breaston. Uncle Don, Auntie Dorothy and Peter moved from 15, Conway Avenue to a new bungalow in Orchard Close, Ockbrook (off Collier Lane). Don was aged about 50 at the time and was still employed by Barrons', as he had been since leaving school in 1925 at the age of 14. Although most of Barrons' business had been closed down and the land sold off (e.g. our Kimberley Road cricket field), they still had odds and sods here and there and Don spent his days tending the rose fields in Ockbrook. Roses have always been a passion in the Thornton family and that must have been a labour of love for him.

Just when we thought the dust had settled following all this upheaval, we got the dreadful news on June 3rd, 1964, that Uncle Don had collapsed and died, aged 53. He'd been home for his lunch break as usual that day and had mentioned to Dorothy that he didn't feel very well but he went back to work and subsequently collapsed with a heart attack. The alarm was raised when he was late home at teatime and he was found lying amongst his beloved roses. The news circulated quickly and everyone was in shock, none more so than Nana, who never came to terms with his death. There can surely be no greater ordeal for any of us than having to attend the funeral of one of our own children. Over the following 18 months, there was a marked decline in her well-being and the Doctor was of the opinion was that it was almost certainly a consequence of grieving and was psychosomatic rather than physical. Nana had seemingly lost the will to live and she took to her bed during the last few weeks of her life and that's where she died on January 31st, 1966, aged 80.

Carole and I left School in June, 1963, after sitting A and O-Levels respectively. On September 3rd, 1963, I started work in the Rolls Royce Apprentice Training School, Ascot Drive, Derby, spending two years there. I was then transferred to the Burner section (Dept 0490, No 0 Shop) in the Main Works, where I stayed for 4 months. It was while assigned to this Department that I promptly became acquainted with the dubious pleasures of working the nightshift. I transferred to the Shafts section in

January, 1966, (Dept 0481, No 4 Shop), only to find that they were just about to begin the process of moving machinery, personnel, and all, down to No 1 Shop. The move took about 6 months and was completed by the summer of 1966 and I spent 12 years there before leaving the Company in 1978. I was privileged to serve as Departmental Shop Steward for one year in 1974 and I also made an unsuccessful bid for promotion during that same year. Although it was a bit of a wrench, I made the decision to terminate my contract with RR and left the Company on Friday, June 2nd, 1978. I started a new job as a Dairy Roundsman at GNCS, Meadow Lane, Long Eaton on Tuesday, June 6th, 1978, where I remained until I retired on medical grounds in January, 1998.

Carole had joined the staff at the National Provincial Bank, Market Place, Long Eaton in July, 1963 and was in their employ until January, 1972, by which time she was 7 months pregnant with Richard. At the time she left the bank, it was in the process of merging with the Westminster Bank and subsequently came to be known as the Natwest Bank. Somewhere along the way, we decided that Saturday, June 8th, 1968, would be our wedding day and the ceremony was to take place at the Wesleyan Church, Derby Road, Long Eaton. Following the wedding service, Carole's parents Jim and Hetty hosted a small family reception at their home at 121, Bennett Street, after which, Carole and I moved into our first marital home at 90, Wilsthorpe Road, Breaston. This property was formerly a large detached house which had recently been converted into 4 flats and we took up residence in Flat 4 on the ground floor. We were now next-door-but-one neighbours of Uncle Stan and Auntie Edna who had previously moved to No 86, as already mentioned. Small world, ain't it? Once I had finally flown the nest, Mum, Dad, Kathleen and Tonka were then able to make the move to their new home at 141, Taunton Avenue, Whitleigh, Plymouth in May, 1969. This move had been in the pipeline for some time but was delayed for various reasons.

We had planned to rent the flat for two years, thinking that would be ample time for us to become adjusted to the new routine of married life. It would also give us the opportunity to search at our leisure for a suitable property to buy. Once we had reached that stage, maybe then we could think about starting a family? For quite a while prior to our wedding, I had been working the nightshift on a voluntary basis, though the Lord only knows why. Once we were married, of course, that meant leaving Carole home-alone all night, which, in hindsight, seems ridiculous. She had been used to having a budgie as a pet when she was at home and so I decided to buy one as a 24th birthday present and, as the six-week-old chick was a boy we named him "JAMIE". We used to spend hours talking to him and he very soon picked up a repertoire of phrases so comprehensive that we could almost hold a conversation with him. That little bird turned out to be an absolute gem, so good natured and endearing and he was a most welcome addition to the family.

I had passed my driving test in April, 1966, at the second attempt and within weeks had acquired a 12-year-old Austin A30 (VRB 677) which, it has to be said, was in need of some attention. My brother Ken and I towed it from his brother-in-law's house in Sawley back to Borrowash, where we set about stripping down and rebuilding its seized engine. This task kept us occupied for many of the winter evenings of 1966/67 in his perishing shed at 71, Kimberley Road, but we completed it and the car was back on the road by the spring of 1967, complete with MOT. We did have a problem with the brakes pulling to one side but that was eventually solved with some expert help from Charlie Sutton on Canal Street.

When we started out on this exercise, I knew absolutely nothing about car engines but I do now, thanks to Ken's patience and guidance. By the spring of 1969, we had been driving the A30 for a couple of years and its 850cc engine had served us well but, sadly, it now seemed to be burning more oil than petrol. This was despite the fact that John Gregory and I had replaced the piston rings along the way. We decided to put the car out of its misery and replaced it with a 4-year-old Austin 1100 (GUV 175 C), which we bought from Newtons of Stapleford for £395.

In the New Year, 1970, new neighbours moved into the flat next to us in the guise of 21-year-old Alan and his pregnant wife, together with their old Jaguar Mark IX, which he was in the process of reconditioning. One Sunday afternoon in April, there was a knock on the door and Alan's wife, who was in a bit of a state, asked if we could help "because Alan has had an accident in the garage". I had noticed him working on the car in one of the 4 open garages on the premises and when she appeared at the door, alarm bells started to ring. I made my way across the yard where

I found him lying on his back with the upper part of his body underneath the car and his legs protruding from the passenger side. He was motionless, with no physical or verbal response and as I knelt down, I could see what appeared to be blood trickling across the garage floor. From the position he was in, it appeared to me that he had gripped the chassis member with both hands in an attempt to haul himself underneath the car but, in fact, it had toppled off the single-point jack which was supporting the front end. I think his head had been trapped between the underside of the 2-ton car and the concrete floor of the garage and he was probably already dead.

Fortunately, there was a telephone kiosk by the front gate from where I rang 999 and I had hardly put the phone down when the ambulance crew arrived from the local station on Briar Gate. They insisted that they should take charge of the situation and so, having already seen enough, I withdrew and left them to it. Even now, this incident fills me with horror because it is a shocking example of how devastating a moment's lapse in concentration or an error of judgement can be. For Alan, tinkering with the old car was a hobby but on that Sunday afternoon, his passion was his undoing and in an instant his life was over.

CHAPTER 4

We made a start on our house-search in the spring of 1970 and it was over before it began, really. We liked the look of 9, Meynell Road, Long Eaton, one of only a couple of properties that we had viewed. It was set in a pleasant-looking area on the SE extremity of the town, with open farmland as far as the River Trent, which is about three quarters of a mile away to the east. About 50 metres from the property to the S, there was a large pond which was stocked with tench and bream mainly but the star attraction had to be the 20lb common carp. Since those days the farmland has been developed with row-upon-row of houses and the carp is probably long dead but the pond, at least, remains largely unchanged.

Our prospective new home was built in 1966 and had been occupied previously by two different families, neither of whom stayed long enough to even make a start on the garden, or so it seemed! The interior wasn't much better and needed decorating throughout from top to bottom in order to cover the existing colour scheme of powder blue, pillar-box red and orange. The back garden, measuring 25 x 9 metres, contained only a concrete coal bunker which was sited directly below the kitchen window. There was no garage, no shed, not even a garden path and the whole area was a jungle of waist-high docks.

Our neighbours Ivan and Jean Gunnell at No 11 soon made themselves known to us and gave us a seemingly pleasant welcome. They had a 3-year-old daughter when we moved in and on occasion we were asked to babysit, which we didn't mind. Jean used to hang their extra washing on our line and preferred to use our phone rather than the public telephone box just around the corner. This continued, especially after the birth of their second daughter in the summer of 1971, until the early 1980s, by which time the girls were of an age when they no longer needed a babysitter. As far as the Gunnells were concerned, that meant the end of our "friendship" and they chose to cause a rift between us over nothing. We'd proved to be useful to them and had served our purpose but now that they had no further need of our services or friendship, we were effectively sacked. Subsequently, we were alienated and treated like second-class citizens, as we still are to this day. Over a period of 35 years, they have dreamt up numerous ways of demonstrating just what vindictive, opportunistic and spiteful tossers they actually are. Sadly, Ivan died on April 9th, 2016, and his highly educated (to use her own self-description) widow Jean is now just another old woman living on her own with no neighbours to talk to.

With the paperwork completed and one or two loose ends tidied up, we took up residence on August 1st, 1970, and could now make a start on turning the house into a home. The land at the back needed to be cleared, dug and levelled, so Thicko Thornton reached for his spade, can you believe, and set about it – what a prat. I can remember digging it but can't remember how long it took but we got there in the end and could now begin the process of creating something that resembled a garden. A garage, a shed, a patio, a lawn and a path are fairly basic garden features but we had none of these, as yet. During September, Mum and Dad arrived from Plymouth – they were itching to see our new house and the area and Dad was keen to help sort the garden. Carole's Auntie Pat (Jim's sister) and Uncle Sam were also due to arrive from Ottowa, Canada, on their first trip to the UK.

For a couple of months I had been feeling a bit under the weather and one night whilst at work, the Foreman (Ken Lewington) asked if I was feeling all-right. Obviously, he could sense that I wasn't my usual self and he suggested that I "knock off" and go home to bed. I think it was about midnight when I got home and as expected, Carole was in bed and, despite my efforts not to disturb her, I think she had woken almost instinctively. She was aware that I hadn't been feeling well of late and, as we lay in bed trying to work things out, I just broke down. I made an appointment to see Dr.Christie at Breaston surgery and he listened as I tried to describe my symptoms. He didn't carry out any physical examination but asked about recent events in my life and ultimately, his opinion was that I was run down and suffering from mild depression and prescribed medication.

This condition was serious enough to have me worried so his diagnosis came as something of a relief because my imagination had told me that it was something more sinister. I suppose it had been quite hectic for the both of us for a couple of years, what with the wedding, moving away from our family homes, Alan's tragic demise, taking on a new house, and all this whilst working nights. I was off work for 6 weeks and on my return in mid-October on the dayshift, Ken suggested that perhaps I could give the nightwork a miss, at least for the time being.

Our guests from Plymouth and Ottowa arrived during my lay-off which meant that I had more leisure time to spend with them. Kathleen had given this trip a miss because, within a few months of moving to Plymouth, she had struck up a friendship with Harry Rosevear, one of the local lads. Choosing not to let the grass grow under their feet, they were married on June 22nd, 1970. Following Mum's death on November 7th, 1980, they eventually decided to move back to Kathleen's roots in 1985, initially to Spondon. They then moved to Darley Dale, where they lived for a dozen years before moving to their present home in Ashford in the Water in 2020. I think that it was perhaps the employment prospects in the South West in the early 1980s and also the ever-diminishing family ties that were the most significant factors in their decision to move north but that is only my guess. Their sons Jonathan, Simon and Michael have all settled in the Matlock area and now have families of their own.

Mum and Dad were our guests for as long as they wanted to stay. Pat and Sam were guests of the Camden Hotel on Nottingham Road and they had decided to hire a Ford Granada limo for use as a runabout whilst they were here. We spent time with Het and Jim showing Pat and Sam the delights of the town, while Dad was itching to make a start on the front garden. When we reached the stage of levelling and seeding the lawn and he suggested that we should bury some crocuses and snowdrops here and there. The crocuses survived for a few years but the snowdrops have spread and still appear each year, just as though they are in God's little acre – nice one Dad.

I was a bit lethargic due to the medication I was taking, to the point where I was nodding off whenever I sat down – that probably explains why the tablets are called tranquillisers. Carole and I had seen a brass-topped occasional table with carved wooden legs in a shop downtown and we pointed it out when we were on walkabout. Pat and Sam had obviously been back to the shop because on their next visit, they presented us with that same table "as a belated wedding gift". That was a pleasant surprise in itself but there was more to come by way of an invitation to visit them in Canada for three weeks next year. We could hardly believe what we were hearing and what a tonic – roll on next spring! Our plan had always been to try to start a family once we'd moved into our own home but, in the circumstances, we decided to delay that for a while.

By the beginning of October our visitors had gone their separate ways and I was due back at work following my sick leave. Although the Canada trip was still eight months away, the thought of it was giving me butterflies because neither of us had flown before and it was a 7-hour flight from Heathrow to Montreal. Carole seemed OK, I was feeling a lot better and we'd had a nice time with Pat and Sam and Mums and Dads. I had been to Borrowash a couple of times to watch the Vics play on the new pitch at Deans Drive and, of course, I let myself be goaded into turning up at the "training sessions" at Spondon House School. This was supposed to be outdoor 5-a-side on the floodlit, tarmac tennis courts, except that the lights were never switched on. We were reduced to stumbling around in the semi-darkness of the nightlights trying to kick anything that moved, the prime target being Tommy Keogh because he usually had the ball! It was great to be mixing with proper footballers like Keogh, Kellogg, Dickenson, O'Byrne and Sibley but it was a bit of a traipse from Long Eaton on those chilly evenings and I only went a couple of times. I had no desire whatsoever to start playing again but I was asked if I would help out by playing in goal for the Reserves and I could hardly refuse. I played only the one game and it was a bit nerve-racking after such a lengthy lay-off but we managed to beat LE Grange Reserves 2–1 at Deans Drive. I can't say that I enjoyed it, though it did help to convince me that I was over my health problems.

More sensible ideas to aid my recovery came from Carole's Uncle Cecil, who suggested that we go to Meadow Lane to watch Notts County and also from her Dad Jim, who suggested I try fishing. This was something new to me, but Jim was prepared to put his patience to the test in trying to show me how to go on, so why not? He must have thought I was a good pupil because he persuaded me to join Armorduct Fishing Club – their waters are on the north bank of the Trent at Sawley from Harrington Bridge downstream to the railway bridge. I entered the Sunday morning matches regularly, though I can't recall winning anything, or even catching anything! I preferred pleasure-fishing on the sandbar below the Harrington Bridge, the canal at Shardlow, the gravel pits at Attenborough or the River Soar at Ratcliffe. I was so grateful to Carole, Jim and Cecil and everyone whose understanding and patience helped my recovery, not least of all RR and Dr.Christie, of course.

We decided that the first jobs in the garden should be to lay a path and a patio at the back and a path along the front of the house below the lounge window. The slabs, sand and cement were acquired from, and delivered by, Sugars' the builders' merchants of Mikado Road, Sawley and I made several trips to Spondon power station for bags of clinker to use as bedding on which to lay the slabs. I always knew that the time I'd spent watching Ernie Cope and his mate Joe laying all those slabs on the Estate when I was a nipper might one day prove to be time well spent. An odd one or two have settled a bit over the last 53 years but overall they have lasted pretty well. The plan was that, once the paths and patio were in place, we would then invest in a garage, which would hopefully be up and running before the Canada trip at the end of May. We worked steadily over the winter and, by the spring, we had laid both paths and the patio. The garage and its concrete base were supplied by B & S Sectional Buildings, of Stapleford. That meant that the car could be locked away out of sight and be a bit more secure during the three weeks that we planned to be away.

I am pleased to say that, despite the domestic programme, I was finding time for the fishing and the football. Notts County had a really good side in that 1970/71 season, with the likes of Brown in goal, Brindley, Worthington, Needham and Stubbs in defence, Masson in central midfield and Hateley, Cozens, Nixon and Bradd up front. These technically excellent players formed the spine of the team on the pitch and their legendary manager Jimmy Sirrel was their inspiration on the touchline. This team was far too good for Division 4 and it was no surprise that, with inspirational and technically excellent support from the likes of Cecil and myself, they duly won the Championship by 9 points and were deservedly promoted. They set a Club record for the number of points in a season under the old system when 2 points were awarded for a win and they were undefeated at home. Two years later, season 1972/73, they were runners-up in Division 3 to Bolton Wanderers, thus winning promotion to Division 2. This was achieved with largely the same squad, plus Willie Carlin and goalkeeper Eric McManus.

Following his departure from the job of groundsman at Plymouth Coop in December, 1970, Dad wasted no time in contacting the personnel department at the local Bush No 2 factory regarding the job of groundsman at the sportsfield they were developing. He was told that the project would not be completed until late summer and the staffing requirements had not yet been discussed. When he asked about any other vacancies the reply was negative but he was assured that his enquiry would be noted. He had been making what he considered to be demoralising visits to the labour exchange for 6 weeks and then, out of the blue, Bush contacted him with regard to a vacancy as a night watchman. He was relieved to be going back to work and started his new job in February, 1971.

The job wasn't strenuous at all but the shifts were long and involved making routine checks at certain locations at certain times and switching equipment on ready for when the dayshift started. Mum told me this during one of our phone conversations and I remember saying to her at the time that, considering the state of his health, the stress of night work wouldn't do him any good. In view of the fact that the basic hours were 57.5 hours and 69.5 hours on alternate weeks with only himself for company, it's hardly surprising that there was a vacancy! He had that massive factory to himself all night and he said that the typewriter he'd found whilst doing his rounds meant that, not only did he have the time and the peace and quiet, but he now had the means to make a start on his version of "Memory Lane". This turned out to be another of his iffy jokes because he'd only completed 3 pages when his story was tragically cut short after he suffered a stroke on the evening of Sunday, May 30th, 1971.

Another winter was over, spring was in the air and, though I hadn't managed to win a fishing match, Notts County had managed to win promotion as Division 4 Champions following a terrific season. The Canada trip was looming large and our flight from Heathrow was scheduled for midday on Saturday, May 29th, 1971, and we needed to be at the airport by 10am. We decided that the best way of getting to London in plenty of time was the midnight "Milk Train" from Derby and Jim kindly offered to drive us to the station. From St Pancras we took a taxi to the Air Canada Terminal and it was only just daylight when we got there. After checking in, we were eventually taken to the airport by minibus, arriving with plenty of time to spare.

We spent the best part of two hours in the rooftop viewing areas watching the aircraft as they queued up to take off and land at one of the busiest airports in the world. That was quite an experience in itself for an aerofan like me. Our flight was eventually called and, as neither of us had flown before, we were naturally apprehensive as we were shown to our seats aboard the gleaming, pencil-slim Boeing 707. The weather was clear as we took off west to east before circling around to fly west over the Midlands, the Isle of Man and Ireland, all perfectly visible, ferries 'n' all.

Ahead of us now was 3000-odd miles of the Atlantic Ocean and about 6 – 7 hours flying time to Montreal – perhaps it was time for something to eat and a snooze?

Eventually we made landfall, or to be more accurate it was "icefall" because the coastal waters were frozen over for a considerable distance from the shoreline. We were now at the end of May and the pack ice was beginning to thaw and break up to form mini-icebergs, which were then floating away to melt into the ocean. Using our cheapo Kodak Instamatic, Carole managed to get a shot of this phenomenon from 30,000 feet! Montreal is about 500 miles inland which meant that we were now about an hour away from touchdown by my reckoning. Pat and Sam were waiting for us and after loading ourselves into his "Oldsmobile 98", we had a 70-mile drive to their home in Ottowa. En route, we were extremely fortunate to avoid being caught up in a serious traffic incident, in which it was reported that some vehicles had left the highway, resulting in at least two fatalities.

The area where they lived was open plan and the street was wide but it wasn't particularly luxurious, though I think most of the properties had an outdoor pool instead of a back garden – less mowing and weeding required. It was about 15:00 (their time) when we arrived at their house to be greeted by clear blue skies and the "Indianapolis 500" live on their massive colour TV, which I swear was as big as our car. We spent the first couple of days relaxing in the sun and writing our cards home. Sam was involved in the construction business and his plan for Tuesday morning was to give me a guided tour of some of "downtown Ottowa" and to show me one or two of the projects in which his company was involved. On a typical day, he would usually be "on site" somewhere in the city by 07:00 for a progress update. At 09:00, he would head for his favourite café for coffee and to make his routine call home to check that everything was OK and to collect any messages. Following his call that morning, however, he told me that there was a change of plan and we needed to go home, which suggested that there was a problem of some kind?

Apparently, soon after Sam and I had left home that morning, my brother Tom called from Plymouth to let us know that Dad had suffered a stroke on Sunday evening and the prognosis was not good. Both Carole and Pat were in tears by the time we arrived home and it took a little while for us to absorb the news and to try to think but the decision to return home to Plymouth was a formality. Sam suggested that it might be better to fly from Ottowa to Montreal rather than drive and he immediately set about making our reservations. It was lunchtime by the time he'd secured tickets for the 30-minute flight from Ottowa to Montreal at 19:30, connecting with a flight from Montreal to Heathrow at 21:00. This flight stopped over at Shannon for about 2 hours and we eventually landed at Heathrow at about 10:00 BST on Wednesday, June 2nd. That was the day that Mill Reef won the Epsom Derby and when we mailed the customary cards to Mums and Dads on our arrival in Canada, I'd made a point of reminding him not to miss the race. He wouldn't even have seen the card – diabolical irony?

We eventually arrived at Paddington Station and, after buying tickets for Plymouth, I rang Tom to let him know that our train was due to arrive at 16:30 and he said he would be waiting. I was not at all surprised when he told me that Dad had died at 20:30 on Tuesday without regaining consciousness. This was in the days before mobile phones and so we had no idea what the situation was while we were en route from Canada. The fact that Tom had decided to contact us was warning enough that Dad was probably not going to recover. Tom took care of the arrangements as he seemed to have the knack of dealing calmly and efficiently with these situations. In the meantime, we moved in with Mum for the duration. I didn't go with Mum to see Dad in the Chapel of Rest because I preferred to remember him the way he was. I can't remember much about the funeral either but I do know that I'd never seen so many of the family gathered together under the same roof.

We were back home at Meynell Road by June 10th, I think, and we still had a week of our scheduled 3-week holiday left. We decided that we'd contact our respective employers with a view to going back to work early and postponing the week's holiday until a later date. Neither RR nor the Bank had any objection and it seemed more sensible than being at a loose end at home with no plans and just frittering the time away. The Canada trip was yet another one of a sequence of "firsts" in my life over a three-year period and it was a great pity that it had been cut short in such tragic circumstances. It's ironic the way these things seem to happen when least expected and we never know what's around the corner. Perhaps that's as well or there would be some days when we wouldn't dare get out of bed!

Dad's death didn't really sink in until we'd been home for a couple of weeks and I recall that it was on a Sunday evening when I began to reflect on things and it all came out. It's a pity that we don't get second chances because even now, 52 years on, I sometimes wish he was here to share his thoughts and his opinions, his frustrations and his humour. I shall always hold him in the highest esteem and wish that I'd made more of an effort to get to know him. He had a natural talent when it came to writing letters, solving crosswords and swearing at the TV but when it came to selecting eight draws on the football pools, he was useless. I think I've inherited some of his talents and traits, albeit to a lesser degree, and I'm sure he would have had plenty of ideas on the occasions when I'm searching for inspiration. That brings to mind the first piece of advice that I remember him giving me: "Can't you find something bloody useful to do for a change!"

Losing someone so suddenly made us realise that we should never take anyone for granted simply because they've always been there. Fate seems to have a way of intervening when least expected and our lives are irrevocably changed in an instant when someone special is lost. To quote from Joni Mitchell, "you don't know what you've got 'til it's gone", but by then, of course, it's too late. As I was saying, it was around June 10th back in the real world and at the end of the month, the marriage between my niece Jane Porter and long-time pal Alan Hunt was due to take place at St. Werburgh's in Spondon. I had been invited to do the honours as best man though the Lord only knows why and, despite his concerns over recent events, I assured him that we were still on track. Alan's home on Green Bank, Spondon, became their marital home until, regrettably, they parted company and went their separate ways. I believe that he continued to live there until he died (see obituaries).

Carole and I had been doing our best on the baby front for a couple of months. There was the odd, fleeting moment when I did wonder if this procreation business might become just another chore if something didn't happen soon? By the middle of August, however, we received confirmation from the Womens' Hospital in Derby that Carole's recent test was positive. We could now start buying and knitting and generally gearing up ready for the arrival of our first baby at the end of March, all being well. As the weeks went by Carole was putting on weight and her normally short-cropped hair was now shoulder length and everything about her was bigger and bonnier and she looked really well. She resigned her position at the Bank in December, 1971, and as we progressed through winter into March her normally trim, 8-stone frame was now more like 12 stones. Some did wonder if she may be carrying twins but the Consultant confirmed that there was only one baby and, anatomically speaking, she should be able to cope.

By Sunday, March 26th, there were signs that she was going into the early stages of labour and the Queen Mary Nursing Home advised that she should be admitted. On the Monday, she was put on "the drip" and subsequently had to endure a prolonged and uncomfortable labour experience. By late evening, there was some cause for concern and the midwife made the decision to send for the doctor. Eventually, much to the relief of everyone, Richard John emerged at 01:50 on Tuesday, March 28th, 1972, weighing in at 9lb13ozs. No wonder it was a difficult birth – how Carole managed I'm not sure but the main thing was that she and Richard were both fine. I felt so proud of the pair of them and, for me, becoming a father for the first time was the most exhilarating experience, fuelled by a mixture of pride and relief, I think. I've never forgotten that sky-high feeling and was reminded of the experience when Sean was born on January 24th, 1975.

It was ten days before Carole and Richard were allowed home and it's not until then that you realise that looking after baby really is a full time job. We invited our long-time friend John Gregory to the christening with a view to asking him formally to act as Richard's godfather. He accepted the invitation but, in truth, we've not seen much of John since then. Richard certainly proved to be the proverbial bouncing baby and there was no mistaking his demands for food – strapped in his baby chair, he'd squawk at the top of his voice while his hands and feet whirred in rhythmical unison. He is now 51-years-old and doesn't have an ounce of spare flesh on him!

It was around the time that Richard was born that, quite out of the blue, one of my workmates at RR asked me if I fancied a round of golf. This came as a bit of a surprise, in view of the fact that I was a non-golfer who didn't have any clubs. I told him that I wasn't really bothered but thanked him for the invitation. Geoff Gossage was not a man to be easily deterred, however, as he told me that he was only a novice himself and that I would be able to borrow some clubs from one of the other lads. I quite thought that it would be an end to it when I then told him that, despite being naturally right-handed, I batted left-handed, as I did at cricket and would at baseball. No such luck – he assured me that fellow left-hander Andy Crofts would lend me his clubs and thus, my last escape route was cut off. Then I began to think, why not? Sinfin golf course was only 10 minutes away from work and so we arranged to go one afternoon when we'd finished our shift at 15:00. I somehow managed to get it round in 98, which was very good for a raw beginner, or so I was told. Little did I realise that this round was to be the start of an on/off, love/hate relationship with the game which was to last for 40-odd years.

I happened to mention my golfing exploits to my hairdresser in Borrowash, the lovely Ron Newton, who I knew to be a keen footballer and golfer, and he suggested that I join him and Ken Porter for a round. Everybody in Borrowash knew Ken Porter and Ken knew everybody in Borrowash – he was our personal and friendly insurance expert, the original "Man from the Pru". In those days, Wednesday was traditionally half-day closing for businesses in the Derby area and the pair of them would usually visit one of the local municipal courses for an afternoon's golf. I was hesitant about going with them as I knew that Ron was a member of Erewash Valley GC and I felt a bit out of my depth. He told me that he seldom played at Erewash because he was crap, Ken wasn't much better and nobody would ever guess which of the three of us was a novice? We alternated between Pewit GC in Ilkeston, Allestree GC and Sinfin GC in Derby and we had a few laughs, helping to temper the frustrations which are usually associated with the game. There's nothing more entertaining than watching somebody slowly, but surely, losing his rag! Sadly, I lost touch with both of them after about 1980 and I think Ken died shortly after that. Sadly, Ron died in June, 2010, aged 65, I believe, following a short illness.

When I first started playing golf, I had a persistent slice when using my woods and Ron suggested I phone Erewash and book a lesson with the Club Professional, an Irishman by the name of Mike Ronan. This I did and, with some trepidation, I turned up at the appointed hour. Mike watched me hit a few balls and it didn't take him long to spot the cause of my problem. He explained the difference between what I was doing and what I should to be doing and he suggested a couple of things I could work on to help put things right. He told me to go away and practice and come back and see him again when I felt ready so that he could check on my progress.

I had got into the habit of going to West Park and using the field near "foxy" as a practise area when it was quiet. I tried to work on what Mike had told me, though that's not so easy when there's no one standing over you. We tend to fall into the trap of practising the things we can do, rather than the things we can't, and then wonder why we don't improve? After a month or so, I went back to see Mike and his advice then was to keep doing what I was doing, forget the lessons and just go out and play. He asked if I was a member of a Club and I replied that I hadn't even thought about joining a Club, being a 26-year-old novice. He handed me an application form and said that he would sign it as my proposer and mid-week membership should be a formality. I had already joined Rolls Royce Golf Society because practically all of my workmates who played were members and it seemed a sensible thing to do. As the weeks went by, I came to appreciate what an extremely well organised and vibrant Society it was and getting involved was probably the best move I could have made.

My name was added to the list of mid-week members of Erewash Valley GC in 1974 and it would now be a question of waiting my turn for a vacancy to arise before I could be offered full membership. I was in the queue but I wasn't going to be holding my breath until a sufficient number of full members either died or resigned because that could take years. I entered as many competitions as I was eligible for in an effort to gain experience and improve. I was fortunate enough to rub shoulders with some really good players along the way, including past and present members of the County team. One or two of them were old enough to be my dad but they hadn't forgotten how to play and could teach me a thing or two. I was privileged to play with, and caddy for, the Club professionals Mike himself, Roger Tattersall, Eamonn Darcy and Alun Wardle.

CHAPTER 5

I was lucky enough to visit Cheltenham Racecourse on Champion Hurdle day, Wednesday, March 14th, 1973, to see Comedy of Errors win the first of his two Champion Hurdle crowns. I had seen a couple of his build-up races on TV in the weeks leading up to race and had also seen him race at Nottingham racecourse. There was no doubt in my mind that, barring a mishap, he would win at Cheltenham and I had backed him ante-post several times. The big day arrived and I drove to Derby to meet up with workmates Barry Clark and Mick Darby and the three of us set off in Barry's car. Despite the fact that pre-race discussions on the merits of the runners continued all the way down the M5, I failed to convince them that my stake money wasn't wasted. Comedy did that for me when he cantered up at 8/1 – for me, he had the race won at the top of the hill.

By the spring of 1974, Richard was 2 years old and growing fast when Carole was confirmed pregnant for a second time, just as we had planned. We always reckoned that 3 years between them would be about right for us and them. As the weeks went by, Carole grew ever larger and this pregnancy followed a similar pattern to the first and our second son Sean David eventually emerged on January 24th, 1975, weighing in at 10lbs10oz. We had encountered some delivery problems with Richard but this time Sean was reluctant to respond to the normal post-delivery breathing stimuli and it was a while before he decided to cooperate. Not the smoothest of starts and, as a precaution, he was transferred to the City Hospital to spend his first three days in an incubator where he could be monitored. This was mainly because of concerns regarding the possible effects of his delayed breathing. As it turned out, the main problem was in trying to find an incubator that was big enough! We appreciate how fortunate we are that both Richard and Sean overcame their initial trials with no apparent ill-effects – a bit of a miracle, thank the Lord.

We invited Alan and Jane Hunt to Sean's christening with a view to asking them to act as his godparents and they accepted in their customary gracious manner. Just before Sean's first birthday, we decided to swap our Austin 1100, which I sold to a workmate at RR, for the slightly larger-engined Morris 1300 Automatic (PTV 602 G). We bought this car from Magnet Garage, where I had been a regular customer since moving to Meynell Road in 1970. It was a clean and tidy, 7-year-old car which had been registered to one lady owner from new. On a sad note, it was not long after Sean was born that our lovely little Jamie Budgie died, aged 6½. Since Richard and Sean had become part of our lives, I have to admit that little Jamie had been neglected and had taken to squawking to gain attention. We'd moved him from the lounge to the kitchen and we used to drape a cover over his cage in an effort to quieten him when, in fact, I should have been giving him the attention that he was craving. Even now, it almost reduces me to tears when I think that I could have behaved in such a despicable and selfish manner towards that lonely little bird. Losing him in that way must rate as one of the saddest episodes of my life.

The summer of 1976 was one of the warmest on record and by the time we took our holiday in the September, we had seen no rain for about 2 months. Richard was 4½-years-old and Sean was just 20 months when we decided to drive to Great Yarmouth to spend a week in a self-catering chalet at California Sands Holiday Park, near Caister. It was a 4-hour drive and after checking in at lunchtime on the Saturday, we were promptly shown to our cosy home-from-home. Unpacking and food-shopping were useful ways of helping us to familiarise ourselves not only with the chalet but also with the prominent landmarks of the surrounding area. We spent some time on that first day trying to plan to make the most of our week with little trips here and there and decided that the best way to start would be to spend our first morning on the beach.

It was just a short walk away and we arrived bright and early after breakfast on the Sunday to claim a suitable spot where we could spend an hour or two enjoying the glorious holiday weather. Our plans were soon dashed, however, because within the hour the weather broke and the rain came down, forcing us to take shelter. Thus, the 2-month drought came to an end on the first morning of our holiday and it hardly stopped all that week – unbelievable! One of our trips was to Lowestoft, about 10 miles down the coast, where we parked the car near the harbour and sat and watched the rain come down for an hour before giving up. I was a keen armchair follower of horse racing in the 1970s and as we were only a couple of miles from the Great Yarmouth track, I decided to spend an hour there on the Wednesday afternoon.

The following morning, Thursday, I was up early and decided to go for a stroll to the beach. As I made my way onto the sand, I looked left and right and it stretched as far as the eye could see in both directions. I wasn't going far as I was already starting to think about my breakfast, but I decided to turn right, scanning the beach ahead and the ocean to my left as I ambled. My attention was drawn almost immediately to something on the sand about 100 metres ahead of me and the closer I got, the more the object began to resemble a person. That thought triggered the adrenalin but I calmly reassured myself that it must be a tailor's dummy, you silly dumpling. I looked around, half-hoping that the "Candid Camera" team might break cover but there was no sign of anyone, not even a dog-walker. The "dummy" was lying face down and appeared to be wearing a vest, plimsolls and shorts, which were down around the ankles. I approached very cautiously to within about 20 metres and it was then that I realised that it was indeed a person and the inanimate posture, the silence and the pallid appearance told me that it may even be a corpse.

I had seen enough and decided to retreat and report back to the chalet before contacting the police. They were quickly on the scene and after showing them to the site, I left them to it. They came to the chalet later to take my statement and we were told that the unfortunate young man had been reported as missing the previous evening. He was one of a party of visitors from a School for Special Needs somewhere in Yorkshire and it seemed that he had found his way to the beach and entered the water in the darkness. Taking into account my statement and the fact that there was no suggestion of foul play, they said it was most unlikely that I would have to return to Yarmouth to attend the inquest. Amen.

I had scoured every instruction book that I could find in Long Eaton library at least twice in my unquenchable thirst for information on the fundamentals of a decent golf swing. I spent many finger-blistering hours on the practice ground, sometimes hitting 300 balls in a session. I entered as many of the midweek competitions as I could at Erewash and I was also involved in the busy schedule provided by the Rolls Royce Golf Society. Their activities took me to the best courses in the area playing with, and against, all sorts of people. I recall being selected to represent the Society in a match at Ashbourne GC and my partner on the day was Bill Ottewell. He was a draughtsman approaching retiring age and a real gent born of the "old school" and one of the Ashbourne pair that we played against was none other than the Governor of Sudbury Prison! The Society Captain's Day was always held on the first Monday in September, RR's "long weekend" and the four in which I took part were held at Mickleover, Kedleston, Cavendish and Hollinwell. My involvement with the Society came to an end when I chose to leave the Company on June 2nd, 1978.

During 1981, our 1300 had begun to develop gearbox problems and we decided to exchange it for an 8-year-old Vauxhall Victor 1800 Automatic (PXD 971 L), once again courtesy of Magnet Garage. It was a bit scruffy around the edges but a sturdier motor. By 1983, my golf handicap was down to 7, an achievement of which I was very proud, especially at Erewash. There was a group of regulars who used to turn up at about noon on Mondays and Wednesdays to play the first 6 and the last 4 holes, commonly known as "the loop". Depending on how many turned up, the day's format would be decided on the first tee, usually after much haggling over partners and shot allowances. Mike and I played together a few times over the years and I always regarded that as a privilege. I would always relish the chance to play with any Pro but Mike could be a rather vociferous character if things weren't going our way and he wasn't one to hide his feelings.

On what must have been one of the last occasions that he and I teamed up, I recall missing a 3-foot, downhill putt on what was the 17th in those days (the Road Hole). Had I holed it, it would have clinched the match against Eamonn and John. Though it was by no means an easy putt, I was annoyed that I'd missed it and the ribbing that I got from the others as we walked to the 18th tee didn't help at all. We played our way in and I promptly put my clubs away and left the group for last time and over the next few months, I think I ventured onto the course only once, by myself. It was customary practice for the Club to issue membership renewal reminders, together with confirmation of the fees due. I decided that £360 for a single round of golf did not represent good value for money for me and that was the end of my Erewash career.

After leaving RR, I started a new career as a Roundsman at the Greater Nottingham Cooperative Society Dairy Department, Meadow Lane, Long Eaton on June 6th, 1978. This change meant a drop in salary but that was partially offset by the reduction in my daily commuting mileage from 25 to 4. By nature, I had always been an early riser and "up with the lark" but after five years of the seemingly relentless 03:00 alarm call, I was beginning to flag and I had neither the energy nor the inclination for golf. I think the truth was that I'd grown tired of the game and needed a break from it and decided to take it at the first excuse. In the summer of 1984, by way of a change, the lads suggested that we try our hand at fishing on Barker's Pond at the end of the street. We cobbled together some of Jim's redundant tackle from the garage and off we went. It proved to be a popular diversion and we made further trips to Trent Lock, the Soar at Ratcliffe, the canal at Shardlow and Attenborough gravel pits. Looking back, we were lucky that none of us fell in because I can't bloody swim!

By 1985, the Vauxhall was well past its best and we scrapped it in favour of an Austin Princess 2200 Automatic (BCH 632 T), which we bought from a chap in Sandiacre in a private sale. I've no doubt that this was a really nice car when new but I'm afraid that by the time we bought it, I discovered all too late that it was absolutely rotten underneath, particularly at the back end, including the suspension, petrol tank and sub-frame. I should have been more thorough when viewing it but it was only 7 years old and it never occurred to me that it would have deteriorated so quickly into such dreadful condition. I had been foolish enough to buy this deathtrap and was fortunate indeed that it had not been the cause of a serious accident. John at Magnet Garage did his best to patch it up as parts of it collapsed but it was a forlorn task. As I have already described, we scrapped it in favour of the Capri in an "out of the frying pan into the fire" manoeuvre in 1990.

By way of putting things in perspective, we had the extremely sad news in October, 1988, that my half-sister Sheila had died, aged 59. The funeral service was held at Markeaton Crematorium, Derby, followed by a "doors open to all" reception at 36, Kirkdale, which was typical of Sheila's way of doing things. I recall part of the message I wrote to go with her flowers: "You taught me my first swear words and I haven't forgotten any of them". All the family were there to say their goodbyes but I haven't seen, or heard from, any of the Porters in the 35 years since.

Riverside Junior Football Club was founded in 1981, based on the principle of providing kids up to the age of 16 years with the opportunity to play against teams of their own age group. Those who were blessed with any sort of ability were usually snapped up by the more ambitious clubs and those who weren't quite so talented were lucky to find a club that wanted to give them a game. Riverside Juniors was all about giving these youngsters the chance to get out on the pitch and play, regardless of their ability, or lack of it. Sean registered to play for the Club in 1985 when aged 10 and almost immediately made his debut for the Under-12s. It was standard practice that parents were invited to help out in some capacity, such as providing transport on match-days and supporting on the touchline to start with. With any luck, the more enthusiastic ones might eventually be tempted into serving on the Committee – I believe this process is known as regeneration.

Out of a team of 11 players, we were lucky to see 2 or 3 parents who were prepared to give of their time on Sunday mornings and there was usually a shortage of volunteers and transport, but we always seemed to manage. This was how we became involved with the Club in 1985 – Sean was the footballer and I was both taxi driver and supporter and before long, I was helping out at training as an unofficial assistant to Alan Buxton, the Under-14s manager. He was a good man who was blessed with more than his fair share of patience and I like to think that we worked well together. There was never any shortage of effort from the players and it was disappointing, for their sakes, that we couldn't manage to win more often.

To cut a long story short, I was eventually approached by the Committee with a view to taking up the position of Club Secretary. After some discussion with Carole, we decided to accept the challenge and I was officially appointed at the AGM in March, 1986. With 6 teams (U11s – U16s), 120-odd registered players, 100 other clubs at various age groups in the Derby City Junior Leagues and other institutions to liaise with and cater for, it was a multi-faceted, time-consuming job which didn't attract too many applicants. Nobody seemed to stick it for long and I have to admit that there was some trepidation on my part when I started but I took my time getting used to things and trying to simplify the system.

Fortunately, things went well for me in the beginning, my confidence grew by the week and I was soon on first-name terms with just about everyone that I came into contact with, including the League hierarchy. There would be mail and phone calls to deal with on most days and it was certainly a busy job which you needed to get on top of, and stay on top. In retrospect, I wonder how I ever had the time to go to work. I feel both proud and privileged to have served in the job for 3½ years, during which time the Club expanded from 6 to 8 teams with the addition of the U10s and U18s. After his final season with the U16s in 1990, Sean went on to play in goal for both Reprobates and Independiente in the Long Eaton Sunday League before putting his football career on hold while he was at University from 1993-96.

There had been one or two decisions made in Committee which I disagreed with and could not support and I was tiring of the politics which was becoming increasingly more prevalent in meetings of late. From my point of view, I had enough to do as it was and didn't really appreciate the negative interference from one or two individuals. They seemed bent on nit-picking and throwing spanners in the works, while seemingly in pursuit of their own agenda. My patience had worn thin and that was becoming a distraction and I thought that perhaps the time was right for change. I therefore gave the Club one months' notice of my intention to stand down, as of September 6th, 1989, by which time I'd had a meeting with my lady successor to hand over all the paraphernalia and to offer advice, should she need any.

I have no idea how she coped, or for how long, but I know that I relished the involvement and enjoyed carrying out my Secretarial duties. I shall always be grateful to Riverside Juniors for giving me that opportunity, though I never got to know how they rated me as a Secretary. The positive aspects of the job far outweighed the negatives but I felt that the time was right for change. The overall experience was an eye-opener that I wouldn't have missed for the world.

Since those days, Riverside FC has continued to grow, even to the point where the Club now has a team playing in senior football, I believe, thus abandoning the principle on which it was founded. The Club must now be one of the biggest in the Midlands, with some 28 teams playing in various leagues, or so I read, and I should very much like to know how they cope with the administration. I should also like to know what became of the 6-a-side football tournament which we launched at Wilsthorpe School Sports Hall in April, 1989, under the name of "The Riverside Salver". Initially involving 3 age groups, U10s, U11s and U12s, it ran like clockwork over 3 successive Sunday afternoons and proved to be very popular with everyone involved and on all three Sundays, Councillor Bill Camm came along to present the trophies. I seem to remember reading that it was subsequently included in the programme of events at the now defunct Long Eaton Festival as an outdoor tournament. I should like to pay tribute to my right-hand man, the human dynamo that was Tony Duncan, for his tireless effort and overall support as Assistant Secretary, but particularly with regard to his work on the "Salver".

By 1985, CWS had taken over control of the GNCS Dairy Department and by 1991, Dale Farm had taken over control from CWS. We all knew that this would almost certainly mean the introduction of their franchise system. They lost no time in foisting it upon us amidst an avalanche of propaganda and those of us with mortgages to pay had little choice but to sign up, which I did in June, 1991. I felt that we were steamrollered into the idea and many of the roundsmen who were there when I started rejected the change and left. I didn't like it from the start and once Dale Farm had got their feet under the table, the atmosphere was dreadful. As franchisees, our official status was "self-employed" and as such, we were solely responsible for dealing with our own tax affairs, etc., which meant engaging the services of an accountant. At the same time, we weren't allowed to forget the fact that we didn't actually own the rounds or the business because Dale Farm retained all the rights whilst off-loading the responsibilities. We were subjected to relentless pressure and generally treated like shit by the Dale Farm people. This included some of their roundsmen who had transferred to Long Eaton from their Beeston depot – arrogant beyond belief and they were only bloody milkmen! I grew to hate the regime and the attitude which they had brought with them and spent as little time as possible in the depot.

If all that wasn't enough, we had to put our adopted cat "GYPPO" to sleep on August 3rd, 1991, but I can't blame Dale Farm for that – his demise was due to a combination of cat 'flu and kidney problems. Within a matter of 3 or 4 days, our other adopted stray cat (we'd named him "MAGPIE" because he was black and white) cautiously came into the lounge for the first time and he seemed to sense that Gyppo was not coming home. After taking a good look round, he promptly jumped up onto the sofa and began to wash himself, as if to say, "I think this is mine now".

The one bright spot amidst all the gloom was that Sean had been helping me on the milkround on Saturdays and he'll never know how much that was appreciated. He liked the job and enjoyed meeting the customers and with his help, the extra work involved in loading up, doubling up and collecting on Saturdays took on a whole new complexion. It didn't take long for him to get the idea and it worked like clockwork with the two of us and, after a later 04:00 alarm call, we were usually home by 10:30am and, dare I say, it was almost a pleasure? On the occasions when I had to work Saturdays on my own, it was a real trial with the usual 03:00 alarm and not getting home until 13:00. It was too much for one man and pretty well all of the roundsmen had an assistant on Saturdays.

It was during 1990 that I inadvertently got involved with Ganleys Snooker Club, which was situated above Burtons the tailors in Long Eaton High Street. Sean had been offered a little job brushing the tables and, due to my long-established wariness of these places which originated during school days, I went along with him for a game and a recce. I was introduced to Margaret, who I took to be the manageress – she was Irish and may well have been a Ganley. I also met Jim, who appeared to be friendly with Margaret, though I'm not sure about their relationship. One thing led to another and before I knew it, I had been elected captain of the 'C' team, which played in the local snooker league. This team consisted of 5 or 6 lads not unlike Sean, but they were a bit undisciplined and somebody had the idea that I might be able to give them some guidance in that respect. They didn't need convincing of the fact that I couldn't play snooker but they did need to learn that it might be to the team's advantage if they were to turn up regularly for matches. If they were unavailable for selection for any reason then perhaps they ought to let someone know?

The short winter season ran from September, 1990 until January, 1991. We managed to honour all of our fixtures, despite one or two of the players dropping out along the way. I managed to recruit Richard to our ranks to help out when we were short-handed but he seemed to enjoy it and became a regular in the team. I must admit that it seemed rather odd to see three "Thorntons" listed in a team of 5! Despite my misgivings, I think we enjoyed our first season in the snooker league overall and that's just as well because it was to be our last. Within a few days of me forking out £30 for 3 annual Club subscriptions for 1991, we found that the premises had been locked and sealed and all who sailed in them had vanished. Ganleys had closed its doors without notice, with immediate effect and I had been conned out of £30. I also lost my £10 cue, which was stored behind the bar when not in use. My scepticism regarding these dimly-lit dives had proved to be well founded but, despite the fact that I'd had my doubts, I was annoyed that I'd still fallen into the trap.

Sean passed his driving test in November, 1992, and six months later he'd also passed English, Geography and Psychology at A-level, which meant that he would be University-bound come September. He was by no means a regular player and didn't have any clubs but he said he fancied a round of golf at Trent Lock at some stage during the summer holidays. Despite the fact that my clubs had been in the garage for 10 years, they appeared to be in reasonable condition and we now needed to sort out some clubs and a bag for Sean. The best way to solve that was to go and see Mike at Erewash – job done. I was quite looking forward to the challenge of trying to hit a golf ball again after my 10-year lay-off. Sean took to it like a duck to water, as is his wont with most things he tries, but I think it was a case of "one good one, one bad one" for both of us, which is probably all that we could expect.

I can't remember how many times we played but suddenly, another summer had gone and September was upon us – time for Sean to depart for Staffordshire University, Stoke, to begin a 3-year course in media studies. His partner at that time, Helen Fryer, had enrolled at Birmingham University for her course and, sensibly, they decided to share student digs in the quiet Birmingham suburb of Balsall Heath. Carole and I visited them there a few times and it seemed quite a pleasant area with good neighbours and was certainly a stark contrast to the busy, heaving city. He completed his course in June, 1996, gaining a 2:1 BA degree in Film, TV and Radio Studies. His Graduation Ceremony took place at Trentham Gardens in the following October – a very special day for everyone.

CHAPTER 6

Richard passed his driving test in March, 1990 and left school in June of that year after passing Art, History and English at A-level. He decided against going to university, though he wasn't sure what he was going to do in terms of a job. During the summer holidays, the two of us went to an address in Derby to view a Ford Capri Automatic (TYG 292W) which I had seen advertised in the Derby Telegraph. I think I had bought this car before I had even seen it and it proved to be yet another iffy buy. Even after we'd sorted out its teething problems, I think it must have been the worst car in the world to drive.

Since Easter, 1982, Carole had been working part-time for Hammards Catering Ltd. She was one of about 10 staff who tended to the lunchtime needs of the patrons of the Skill Centre on Wilsthorpe Road, Long Eaton, under the watchful eye of the Catering Manager, John Harrison. Things were fine and then in 1990 it was announced that the Centre was to close as a training facility but would remain open as a rehabilitation centre. Inevitably, Hammards lost quite a few of their customers and had little choice but to pull out. This meant that John and his staff were left to cope with whatever was left of the business and to wonder just what the future had in store. John gathered his staff together in a "caterers' huddle" to tell them that he was prepared to try to keep the ship afloat but he wouldn't be able to do it without the support of the crew. His challenge was accepted and the business was renamed "New Venture" but it soon became apparent that it was going to be a struggle just to make ends meet. Over the next few months, despite the added attraction of the revamped canteen, customer numbers fluctuated from one week to the next and the staff gradually dwindled away to seek pastures new.

By the summer of 1990 John, Carole and Jan were the only survivors from the original team and on odd days, lunchtime with just the three of them could be a bit hectic. Sometimes they needed an extra pair of hands and Richard was only too willing to help out. They were busy in patches but not making enough money overall and John told Carole that he could no longer afford to pay the wages for her extra hours and if she decided to move on, he would understand. It was time to call it a day and, having left on the best of terms with John, she began trawling through the "situations vacant", applying for any job that she thought she might be capable of doing. One of these applications came up trumps and in September, 1990, she started a new job at the Driving Standards Agency in Nottingham.

This was a Civil Service position and initially she was employed on a temporary 6-month contract before being promoted to the full-time staff in June, 1991. In the meantime, John had also decided to call it a day at the Centre and retired to the pub, whilst Jan decided to go back on the game. John lived near the County Cricket Ground in Derby and we never saw or heard from him again until some years later. Quite by chance, I happened to read in the Derby Telegraph obituary notices that he had died on January 20th, 2015, aged 82. He had often been heard to say that he'd like to see his name in the paper one day but I don't think he meant on that bloody page!

In the meantime, Richard had signed on at the local Employment Agency, from where he was dispatched to all four corners of Long Eaton on various short-term assignments. They were mostly fart-arse little labouring jobs that nobody wanted but they were character-building and all part of life's rich tapestry, as they say. One of these jobs was at Leisure on Meadow Lane, Long Eaton, and after he had finished there and moved on, the Company contacted the Agency with a view to him returning for a second stint. It seemed that he had made an impression and that eventually resulted in the offer of a full-time position in the warehouse. He accepted and joined the payroll in June, 1991, and is still there to this day, having completed his award-winning 25 years of continuous service in 2016. During the past 10 years, a US-based consortium has taken over control of the Company and they are now involved in the manufacture and delivery of AGA cookers. The Company continues to produce quality sinks, now bearing the new Company trademark of "Rangemaster". He is one of a team of five in the warehouse who work a three-shift rota to cover the hours between 06:00 and 17:00, so no nightshifts. He has acquired his forklift operator's licence and also served as the Trade Union Representative during the time he has worked at the Company.

One evening in 1993 whilst out on the town with Sean, Richard was introduced to a young lady by the name of Dawn Pinager. Dawn was in Sean's year at school and she and Richard seemed to get on well and were soon seeing quite a lot of each other. At the time, she was living with her older sister Rachel in Sawley and whenever Rachel was away at university, Dawn was left on her own. It seemed a sensible idea for Richard to move in with her, thereby killing several birds with one stone, and this he did in June, 1993. Carole and I visited them on a few occasions and they seemed to be getting along just fine but, alas, their relationship began to deteriorate. He moved out in February, 1996, and that was the end of that.

By coincidence, Sean and Helen were also going through a bit of a rough patch at that time and they too had decided to split up, just when they were in sight of the finishing line at University. Sean returned home to join Richard, at least for a while until they got themselves sorted out. Helen continued to live in their digs in Balsall Heath which meant that Sean was commuting to Stoke for the rest of that final term. Once their university courses were finished, they arranged to meet at the digs to tidy up and collect their belongings prior to moving out. It was during this rendezvous that they decided to try to patch things up. They'd had a taste of independence while living away in Birmingham and I think it was always their intention to look for a place of their own once their University days were over.

However you do it, this costs money and finding a job was the first priority for both of them. Helen had her heart set on becoming a teacher and was soon enrolled on a one-year course to gain her Post Graduate Certificate of Education (PGCE), which is a mandatory requirement before you can apply for a teaching position. There seemed to be a distinct shortage of jobs that suited Sean's qualifications and he eventually joined Carole on the staff at DSA in October, 1996, which at least guaranteed him a regular income. I was hopeful that maybe his Monday-to-Friday working week would mean that he might be available again to help me on the milkround on Saturdays?

In 1995, I happened to notice that Stephen Palmer's on Tamworth Road were advertising a Metro City (F 55 GRA) – it sounded attractive and so Carole and I went along to enquire. It had been registered to one lady owner from new, had low mileage and it seemed like a nice little car. After a test drive around the block and the offer of a generous discount on the Capri, we decided to buy it. To be honest, it was tinny and a bit "clackity-clack", like 4 ball-bearings in a bucket, but it felt good to be in control again after the Capri, which I think we were glad to see the back of.

In 1997, Sean and 3 of his school pals got together to form the band known as "EXIT", with himself on drums, Michael Tighe on vocals, together with John Pinfield and Kris Brown on guitars. This was family history repeating itself 35-years-on but with two main differences – Exit wrote all of their own material and then went out and performed it in public. They played a few local gigs, a couple of which Carole and I went to see and we were impressed, not only with the music, but also with how much they had progressed in such a short time. They played together for about a year but then Kris was due to go off to university and Michael decided to move back to his native Ireland. The following year saw Kris abandon his university course and on his return he was keen on the idea of trying to revive the band. They adopted a new name, "THE HEIGHTS", but something was missing and it didn't quite work and the band broke up in 2001. The original members of "EXIT" were reunited in 2016 for a weekend of "rehearsals" in the Nottingham studios to celebrate 20 years since the formation of the band.

In the meantime, the hot gossip on the Leisure grapevine seemed to be focussed on Richard and Dawn splitting up. I imagine that he'd probably confirmed the story to someone in confidence but that someone couldn't keep a secret? Sue was one of the ladies on the canteen staff at Leisure who had obviously heard the gossip and she mentioned to Richard that her daughter Samantha (Sam) had been through a similar experience and that she was now on her own. Sam had been invited to a party and was hoping to find a chaperone and Sue suggested that he make her an offer. With Sue acting as the go-between, Richard and Sam met for the first time at the Tappers Harker pub and the outcome of that meeting was that the two of them went to the said party. It is one hell of a coincidence, but as I write this on March 20th, 2018, it is precisely 22 years to the day since that first meeting.

When Richard and Sam first met, her ex-husband was already history but, although he was out of the picture, she was still living in the home that they had shared, together with their 3 children, at Castle Donington. Richard visited them there once or twice in an effort to get acquainted with Christopher, aged 9, Hannah, 6, and Charlotte, 3, in their own surroundings but, inevitably, these visits didn't go unnoticed by the neighbours. It wasn't long before Sam's ex-mother-in-law was turning up to watch the comings and goings at the house, which must have been unnerving, to say the least. In an effort to evade the attentions of this spy, who had also taken to stalking her, Sam and the children moved to her parents' home in Long Eaton in October, 1996. Their house was three storeys and Sam arranged the top floor to accommodate the four of them, with room for a guest as well! The kids appeared to take to Richard from the word go and he's never been anything other than "Dad" to them and he chose to spend most of his leisure time with them.

The stalker was still on the scene, however, and on one occasion Richard and Sam spotted this woman when they were shopping in ASDA. They had tried to ignore her but Richard eventually cracked and confronted her with a verbal volley which brought the shop to a standstill. She promptly took the short walk across the car park to Midland Street police station to report the incident and, to cut a long story short, Richard was summoned before Ilkeston Magistrates on a charge of affray. His solicitor made sure that the history and the full story of the "stalker" was made known at the hearing and the outcome was that Richard was given a 12-months conditional discharge, tempered to some extent with a degree of empathy. The complainant was not present on the day but we thought that the stranger on the back row of the courtroom was probably her eyes and ears. In any event, she disappeared from their lives following the case and hasn't been seen or heard of since.

Sam had applied for a council property before she met Richard and eventually that bore fruit and she and the kids moved to Sawley in June, 1997. Because of the tenancy conditions, I think Richard was restricted on visiting hours to start with because of the technical difference between a visitor, a lodger and a resident. They had to be careful because the very idea that their activities might lead to some muck-raking neighbour jumping to the wrong conclusions was unthinkable. Richard and Sam were determined to change this situation and that meant Sam finding a job of some sort once Charlotte started school. Hopefully, she would then be able to ditch "the system" and regain her independence, thus enabling her to enjoy her freedom and privacy, just like a real person. A few hours at the local Coop started her ball rolling but she was soon on the move to join the lunchtime catering staff at Wilsthorpe School. This meant a few more hours and a bit more money and she could still be at home for the kids when needed. The big move came at Xmas, 1999, when she joined the temporary staff at Asda and this led to her being offered a full time position and, 24 years later, she is still there.

They have planned ahead and worked hard for what they've got, always with the children in mind, and they have made a pretty good team. They spent 19 years planning for their wedding day and the dream was realised when the ceremony took place on Friday, August 6th, 2015, in the picturesque and romantic Devonian village of Mortehoe. Chris, Hannah and Charlotte (1) eventually left home to build their own nests with their respective partners Charlotte (2), Rob and Robbie. Perhaps I should explain that Charlotte (2) is Chris's wife, Rob is Hannah's partner and Robbie is Charlotte (1)'s partner. Richard and Sam are now left to plot a new course on their journey through life, in an effort to balance their time to best effect between work, rest and play and they seem pretty good at that as well.

In the spring of 1997, Richard mentioned to me that he would like to try his hand at golf as his appetite had been whetted for the real thing after playing the computer-game version. We thought that a session or two on the driving range at Trent Lock GC might be the sensible way to start, with a view to learning some of the basics before making any commitment. He made good progress and was keen enough to join the Leisure Golf Society and took part in his first competition with them at Maywood GC in September, 1997. He wasn't over-impressed with the Society's away days, however, as there were one or two folks involved that he couldn't get on with. These were the relatives of Members and these know-it-all guests seemed to turn up solely with the intention of dominating events with their ill-informed criticisms. It didn't take long for him to decide that he preferred hassle-free recreational golf with his mates.

In October, 1997, Sean and Helen decided to make the move to their own home at 35, College Street, Long Eaton, which was very similar in design to Hetty's house on Bennett Street. Sean and I, in the meantime, decided to resume our snooker careers, this time at Potters Snooker Club on Regent Street. Just the two of us on a table in a private room on Sunday mornings trying to put the theory of potting balls into practice but I never quite mastered the art. Potters was on the 2nd floor of the building which is known as Regent Mills and access was via 3 flights of stone stairs – there was a lift but it was too often out of order and not to be trusted. I had been experiencing breathing problems of late and those stairs became more and more of a challenge. I'd been going to work as usual, though it was a bit of a struggle and I found that when I lay down in bed I was virtually suffocating and ended up trying to sleep sitting upright on the sofa. This had been going on for a couple of months and it was obvious that the problem was not going to go away. It had become a cause for concern and Carole insisted that I should go and see the doctor.

We were approaching the week before Xmas, always our busiest time on the milkround, and I said I would try to see that through and then make an appointment. Throughout most of that week, both Carole and Sean were turning out to help me with deliveries – I just sat in the cab issuing instructions while they did the legwork. Even so, by the time we got home on the Saturday, December 28th, I was exhausted and on my knees on the floor. I was close to tears because I knew that I was ill and hospital was beckoning. To allow me to take the Tuesday off, we "doubled-up" on the Monday and when we got home, I rang the surgery and made an appointment to see Dr.Crompton the next day, Tuesday, December 31st, at 16:15. He was rather concerned, not only about the state I was in but also because I had waited so long before going to see him. My vitals were all over the place and he had no hesitation in sending me straight to the hospital. He phoned to let them know that I was on the way and also gave me a letter of introduction to take with me. After going home to collect an overnight bag, we took a taxi to the DRI and were at the reception desk on Ward 4 by 17:45.

During the evening, the duty Doctor gave me a preliminary examination and sent me for a chest X-ray. At around 22:00 Dr Tukan, the Registrar, turned up to explain the results of my X-ray and said that I would need to stay in hospital. Over the next few days I underwent countless tests and eventually the diagnosis was "heart failure due to hypertensive cardiomyopathy". This condition is comparatively rare and can often go undetected before proving fatal, regardless of the victim's age. I was very lucky, considering that I left it so long before seeking treatment. When I was admitted, my blood pressure and heart rate were sky-high and the X-ray showed fluid on my lungs.

Apparently, my heart wasn't pumping as it should because the muscle on the left side is weak – "dysfunctional left ventricle". The Consultant, Dr Millar-Craig, said that diagnosis had proved to be a teaser but the Team finally nailed it and were then able to decide on the appropriate treatment. My condition may have been the result of a minor heart attack which I may not even have been aware of, or the muscle may have been subjected to a viral attack. The most likely cause, however, was that it was genetic. I did not require any invasive treatment but a cocktail of 7 drugs was prescribed in order to reduce my blood pressure and heart rate to an acceptable level, to clear excess fluid from my system and to thin my blood. All this helps to reduce the workload on the heart and over the week, my condition improved sufficiently to allow my discharge as an in-patient on Wednesday, January 7th, 1998.

Following my discharge, I attended Dr.Crompton's surgery regularly, at his request, until his retirement in April, 2002. He said I'd be well looked after as the Practice was about to launch a new initiative in the form of a long-term illness clinic, which I still attend annually. Patients with conditions such as heart disease, diabetes, asthma, etc. are assessed at regular intervals, usually annually, by a specialist nurse who will check blood counts, medication, vital signs, weight and general well-being. Advice designed to help and encourage people in my situation to stay active and delay the inevitable deterioration is also available. I continued to attend the out-patients' clinic at the DRI every 3 months between January, 1998 and February, 2002, when I was finally discharged. I was not fit enough to return to work on the milkround and took early retirement on medical grounds in January, 1998, and haven't worked since. I am now 77 years old and still taking the same cocktail of drugs which the Team prescribed 25 years ago, together with some additional medication which has been added from time to time and this will continue for the foreseeable future. No praise is too high for the Team who looked after me at the DRI and I shall always be thankful for their expertise and dedication.

I had been hospitalised for the first time in my life during the first week of 1998 and it was such a relief to be back home. It took a while for Magpie to work out who I was but after a bit of fuss and a chat, the penny dropped and he was fine. My illness had proved to be a bit of a nuisance, not only because it made Carole's days longer than they already were but it had also interrupted the golf and the snooker and had cost me my job! Visiting must have been a real ball-ache and I'm grateful to everyone who took the time and trouble. Carole turned up every evening straight from work in Nottingham and then she'd got to get home, bearing in mind that we were in the middle of winter. It was probably a relief for everyone concerned that I was only in for a week. After taking a couple of days to find my feet, we thought that the first move should be to let Dale Farm know formally that I would not be returning to work.

I phoned and made an appointment to see the Depot Manager to deliver my letter of notice to him personally, which we did within a few days. He was glad to hear that I was on the mend but was disappointed to be losing someone of my experience. My Supervisor, John Booth, assured me that he would see that the appropriate paperwork was sorted ASAP and he shook my hand and wished me well. Everyone was most understanding and couldn't have been kinder and within a few days I had received all documentation confirming that my franchise agreement with Dale Farm was now terminated, with immediate effect. This meant, of course, that Sean and Alastair (Foulds), who had been doing the round together during my absence, would be relieved of their duties and it would now be up to Dale Farm to fill the vacancy. Alastair's father Peter is not only an old pal from school days but also a near-neighbour and former Roundsman and Supervisor with Dale Farm.

My second career as a milkman was now finally at an end, consigning another phase of my life to history and Carole and I were left to wonder what the future had in store. I was receiving financial support in the form of Incapacity Benefit, which I hadn't actually applied for, and this meant periodic assessment of my fitness to work by independent GPs in order that I could continue to receive this Benefit. We had no way of knowing whether I would eventually be obliged, or able, to return to work, always assuming that a suitable vacancy could be found with a willing employer. As things turned out, I was summoned for assessment only 3 times between 1998 and my eventual statutory retirement in 2011. The third and last occasion was in 2004 and the outcome was that I was told that my next appointment would be 5 years hence in 2009 and I would be contacted in due course. I never heard any more, presumably because by 2009, I was within a couple of years of retirement and deemed to be a case not worth pursuing in terms of time and expense.

CHAPTER 7

Going back to the spring of 1998 and my rehabilitation, Sean and I resumed our snooker sessions and I also ventured to Pewit golf course with Richard, not to play but just to walk the course with him for a bit of exercise. It only takes a couple of hours to play the 9-hole course but the first occasion took its toll and I spent the following day in bed. Dr Crompton later explained that my medication was a fairly potent cocktail and I'd simply overdone things – his advice was to take my time in finding out what I can, or cannot, manage. The weeks went by and I was steadily regaining some strength and confidence, even to the point where I actually played a few holes with Richard at Pewit.

I also ventured down to Trent Lock for an hour on Saturday mornings to watch as the Members played their regular competition. There was a convenient parking area on Lock Lane from where I could view the first green and the second tee. By the end of April, I had been walking a bit, watching a bit and trying to play a bit and could feel the golf bug returning. I suggested to Richard that perhaps we might play a round at Trent Lock, as I wanted to see how I coped on the main course. I suggested that 17:00 on a Sunday evening in May might be a good time. My theory was that, at the tail end of a busy Sunday, most folks would be finished and gone home by that time and there would also be enough daylight left.

I was, to say the least, apprehensive when we turned up to play, wondering how far I would get before I ran out of balls, or steam, or both. About the only thing that I remember about the round was that I managed to complete the 18 holes, despite struggling to put one foot in front of the other on the back nine. By the time I arrived home after dropping Richard off I could barely walk and was using the furniture as a prop to help me get around. Considering the state I was in, I recovered surprisingly quickly over the next couple of days and was ready for another go. I had done surprisingly well for a first outing because the walking involved in playing a full round must be about 3 or 4 miles and I hadn't done that in over 5 months.

I continued my Saturday morning spectating and, with one or two exceptions, the players didn't look to be any more proficient than I was, rusty and out of touch though I may have been. I felt the urge to play competitions again, despite my 15-year sabbatical and the health issues. When I mentioned the possibility of joining the Club to Carole, she suggested I fill in the form and see what happens. I took the completed form to the desk in the Proshop and who should be there but none other than Mr McCausland, passing the time of day with the Staff. We chatted briefly and when I raised the subject of the customary interview he simply said, "You've just been interviewed. Give us the money and you're in". No sooner said than done and I was immediately given a copy of the Club diary, complete with my Membership Code Number, and in August, 1998, I became a fully paid-up Member of Trent Lock Golf Club.

I submitted the obligatory 3 cards for handicap assessment and was allocated what I thought was a very generous 20. I soon found, however, that the course, short though it may be in terms of yardage, had its fair share of quirks in the form of water hazards and 3-putt greens and it took me some weeks to acclimatise. Richard and I managed to play together one morning each fortnight, depending on his shift, and eventually he decided to join the Club, though he wasn't interested in the competitions. I entered most of the Saturday morning competitions and also joined the Seniors Section and entered their competitions on Tuesday mornings. I also played regularly with one of the Sunday morning cliques until I decided to hang up my clubs, playing my last round on Thursday, May 5th, 2005. This was the day I had arranged to play a Senior Knockout match against Mike Molloy. The Competition was known as the MTM Trophy, named after Mike himself, who donated the Trophy and also sponsored the competition. I had made up my mind that, should I lose the match and therefore not be committed to the next round, I would call it a day. Mike deservedly won the match 1–up and that was that and I have to say that I couldn't have wished for more amiable company during that final round. Despite pleas from him and one or two others for me to reconsider my decision, I haven't touched a golf club from that day to this.

I enjoyed my golf at Trent Lock over those seven years and made a few friends along the way but the physical effort was taking its toll and my body was telling me that I had pushed it far enough. I was chuffed that my handicap had eventually come down to 7, as it was 25 years earlier when I was a member at Erewash. The most rewarding aspect was that I felt I had matured into a far better and more consistent player than I was in my Erewash days. I scored in the low 70s regularly on Sunday mornings and it was most gratifying when I eventually managed to reproduce that sort of form in Competition when winning the Ray Booth Trophy on Tuesday, August 5th, 2003. I carded a score of 69 gross playing off a handicap of 11 and I'll never forget the kind remarks made to me by my playing partners and fellow competitors on the day, Tom Lawler and Ray Booth himself.

That was a particularly memorable round for me for all the right reasons but over the next few months there were signs that my game was beginning to taper off. I had inexplicably lost length from the tee and my scores seemed to get progressively higher simply because I was carding too many bogeys. My golf was untidy rather than bad simply because I seemed to lose the knack of scoring. I wasn't prepared to accept second best standards and the message was that, at 59 years of age, my best golfing days were probably behind me and it was time to call it a day.

The weekly rounds with Richard had gradually fizzled out during 2002 for one reason or another and he decided not to renew his membership as he wanted to concentrate on his writing. I retained my membership until 2007 by which time it had occurred to me that, as TL was not a private club, the facilities were open to any member of the public. Therefore, there seemed to be little advantage in paying a membership fee if I was no longer active as a player. I continued to frequent the Club regularly on most mornings and evenings for half an hour's fresh air and banter but I gave that up as well in 2013. Far too many of the folks I met at Trent Lock are no longer here to banter with but memories of them are still so vivid.

Subsequently, I visited the Club only once a year, just before Xmas when the new Club diaries became available. As I was no longer a Member, I had to rely on seeing a familiar face who'd consent to pinching one for me. It would then be added to my collection, which dates from 1998 when I first joined the Club. At some stage, the Club decided to adopt the online data-storing programme and 2018 was the last year that the diary was published in paper form. I don't miss playing at all but it was, for the most part, a pleasure to mix with the Members, including those of the Ladies section when invited, and you won't find a friendlier bunch of people anywhere.

I should like to pay tribute to Edward McCausland, not only for his vision and enterprise in launching the Golf Centre in the first place, but for the diversity and resourcefulness which he has demonstrated over the years in an effort to keep pace with public taste and ever-developing technology. The resilience of this man in the face of adversity was typified in the aftermath of that dreadful night in November, 2000, when the River Trent overwhelmed the flood banks. This left the Riverside course submerged under as much as 10 feet of water and the clubhouse itself, despite being built on raised foundations, was flooded to a depth of 3 feet. Spectacular and scary though the event itself may have been to witness, it must have been heartbreaking to see the efforts of the previous seven years apparently in ruins. I doubt that any such thought ever crossed Edward's mind and, once the flood water had receded sufficiently to allow access, the task of cleaning up, salvaging, replacing and refurbishing began. By the spring of 2001, just 4 months later, the Phoenix rose from the ashes and all departments were up and running again. For weeks after the flood waters had subsided, the hedgerows were littered with debris to act as a reminder of the depth of the flood.

I would also like to make special mention of those individuals who were the founder members of Trent Lock Golf Club. The Club operates from within the Golf Centre premises but is a completely independent and separate business and is run by the Members themselves. It must be gratifying for all those involved in the initial concept to see their groundwork develop into the highly successful and popular Club which it now is, boasting a membership of about 350. The original temporary Clubhouse, a portacabin, was superseded by an impressive all-purpose building, featuring a large Pro-shop, restaurant, entertainment lounges and the latest IT facilities. I doubt that a finer example of a modern, all-under-one-roof Clubhouse could be found anywhere. The Trent Lock complex as a whole has provided endless hours of pleasure for thousands of people over the past 30 years. Quite a few of those folks have been back for more, and that's the measure of its success.

By October, 1997, Sean and Helen had moved to 35, College Street but within a few months their relationship was on the wane and this time it was terminal and in June, 1998, Sean moved into temporary lodgings with a mate. At that point, he wasn't sure about his plans for the future and didn't want to cause any disruption here at home. A colleague at DSA happened to mention to him that she was looking for a lodger to help pay the rent on her home in Bestwood. The idea appealed to him because it meant he would be living in closer proximity to Jo, his new ladyfriend, and also to his job. After deciding to make the move in January, 1999, he and Jo unfortunately went their separate ways early in 2001.

Meanwhile, we decided to change the car in November, 2000, this time for a Rover 100 Kensington (HRB 683 P), which we bought from Lewis' of Long Eaton. This slightly posher version of the Metro City was a nice little car, with metallic claret coachwork and it had been registered from new in April, 1997 to one elderly owner. Sean was glad to have inherited the Metro City because in June, 2001, his Civil Service career was on the move by way of a transfer from DSA in Nottingham to the Derbyshire NHS Communications Office in Chesterfield. He was based at Scarsdale and soon got to know his way around the place and the personnel, especially one particular young lady by the name of Kathryn Tingay. They first met while indulging in mutual fag breaks and soon struck up a friendship and began seeing more of each other out of hours. In December, 2001, he was invited to up sticks from Bestwood in favour of sharing Kathryn's home in Calow, which is a small village just outside Chesterfield. They got along well and, not wanting to waste time, the wedding date was set for September 8th, 2002, with the ceremony and reception to be held at the Priest House, Castle Donington. Nice place and a top do – I'm relieved that I didn't have to foot the bill.

They seemed happy enough as the months went by and in May, 2003, they decided on a move to Bolsover, just 5 miles down the road. They found that they couldn't get on with their new neighbours so moved again in July, 2004, this time to the little village of Woolley Moor, near Alfreton. In September, 2005, we were delighted with the news that they were expecting their first child and James William, our grandson, was born on June 26th, 2006. It's almost inevitable that the initial euphoria surrounding such an event has to make way for the daily responsibilities of attending to the needs of a babe in arms and even the keenest of mums needs a break now and then. Whilst Woolley Moor is close to nature and quaint, there was very little in the way of recreation and no near-neighbours to pass the time of day with. There was a regular bus service but it was infrequent and, with Kathryn not being a driver, they were probably long days when Sean was at work.

As time went on, Kathryn began to feel progressively more isolated and in January, 2011, they decided to leave the idyllic Woolley Moor behind in favour of a move to the comparative bustle and civilisation of Ashgate in Chesterfield. Over the following 18 months, however, the overall situation had begun to put a strain on their relationship and Sean reluctantly decided to move out of the family home in July, 2012. Hetty's former home at 121, Bennett Street, had been vacant since her move to West Hallam in December, 2009, and he took temporary accommodation there. They had been sharing the responsibility for looking after Jim, who was 6-years-old when they separated. When school reopened for the autumn term in the September, Sean found the morning school run from Long Eaton to Chesterfield in the unpredictable traffic to be a bridge too far. That was solved when he and Jim moved to 64, Windermere Road, Newbold, in October, 2012, and this was to be their home for the next 3 years. Meanwhile, divorce proceedings had been initiated and the marriage was finally annulled in February, 2015.

Joint custody arrangements had continued until Kathryn became unwell in the early part of 2013 and was unable to continue to attend to Jim's needs in the way that she would have wished, at least for the foreseeable future. Sean now had to try to sort out a way of keeping all the balls in the air by allowing him to be available for Jim when necessary, as well as continuing to go to work. He devised a cunning plan which meant that, if things worked out, he would take Jim to school every morning except Friday and meet him out on Mondays, Tuesdays and Fridays. Kathryn's parents had offered to meet Jim out of school on Wednesdays and entertain him until Sean called for him after work. The rest of the plan involved Carole travelling to Chesterfield on Thursdays in time to meet Jim out of school at 15:30 and then staying overnight so that she was on hand take him to school the next morning. If all this worked it would give Sean the option of working later on Thursdays or starting earlier on Fridays in order to make up his statutory hours. At a glance, the plan appears complex but it's quite straightforward if you read it slowly. It must have worked satisfactorily because it was in operation for 5 years.

In order to ensure that Jim would be resident within the catchment area for his preferred choice of school at year 6, he and Sean made the tactical move to 25, Schoolboard Lane, Brampton in October, 2015. Jim's school reports are a credit to him and make excellent reading, as they always have, and when it comes to his education, he deserves the best available. Before I continue, I have got "snigs" behind my back as a precaution because none of us know what the future has in store and "snigs" allows me to pass an opinion without the risk of tempting fate. Jim is a talented young man and looks set for a bright future in whatever field he may choose. I am reliably informed that marine biology is a possible option at this point in time and the old Spoonerism, "the oyster is his world" may well turn out to be true. Or, to quote one of the many life-lessons imparted to Terry McCann by Arthur Daley in the TV series "Minder": "The world is your lobster, my son". Jim appears to be a thoughtful and level-headed character and seems to have coped very well with all the toing and froing and the ups and downs but time alone will tell.

Jim had established a routine of visiting his Mum for tea on Monday afternoons after school but, alas, on Monday, September 25th, 2018, he arrived as usual, only to find her prostrate. He had the presence of mind to call 999 but when paramedics arrived, sadly they found that Kathryn was deceased at the scene and they immediately contacted Sean to inform him of the situation. The funeral service took place at Chesterfield Crematorium on October 9th, 2018. Kathryn had a certain fondness for the sea, Whitby being one of her favourite places and Sean, Sarah and Jim paid a visit to the harbour there to commit her ashes to their final resting place. The inquest took place in December and the conclusion was that death was due to natural causes.

Sean and new partner Sarah decided that it must be easier all round for them to live under the same roof in preference to visiting and wasting their lives away sitting behind the wheel of a car. To this end, Sarah sold her house in Sheffield and moved in to School Board Lane with Sean and Jim. They subsequently decided that they needed more space and found what appeared to be the ideal property in Brockwell, only five minutes away from where they were. Sean's house is sold subject to contract and the move depends on the rest of the chain of 6 but they are hopeful that it may happen in October. Considering Kathryn's untimely demise, Jim's ever-growing independence and the new domestic situation involving Sarah, changes were inevitable.

On March 25th, 2002, we had to put our faithful cat Magpie to sleep. Over a period of about 5 years we had made numerous trips to the Vets' for various things, including the amputation of his left foreleg. At the end, the Vet thought that he had a blockage in his bowel and, all things considered, we thought it unfair to subject him to even more trauma. We think he was about 14 years old. I attended a School reunion at the Barge around that time and a second one at Trent Lock in May, 2003. Around 50 former pupils and Staff attended both events.

CHAPTER 8

By 2003, Richard had decided to take a break from golf in favour of a change of direction and he has spent a good part of the 20 years since writing about almost anything which inspired him sufficiently. Examples of his work include a novel about an orphaned fox, a tale based on one of his former schoolteachers and an account of events leading up to the death of Freddie Mercury. As far as I know, he has no particular expertise in any field and the only way to gather info is through research. Efforts to gain the interest of publishers have thus far proved fruitless, though some did keep him dangling for a while before they eventually said no. For the time being, head and brick wall spring to mind.

Following 10 years of effort, one of his most recent assignments focussed on the death of Freddie Mercury and he had high hopes that the 2 years' work he had put into it might earn some recognition but interest was only scant at best. This was a disappointment and it proved to be the last straw and by 2013, he had decided to take a break from writing, mainly because the tit had gone dry, at least for the time being. I doubt that there has been a new story since the Bible was written so perhaps a rehashed old one might do the trick? Considering the tripe that folks buy to make certain folks extremely rich, we are left to wonder just what it is that publishers are actually looking for. It is to be hoped that something, or somebody, will inspire him to pick up his pen again at some point.

Coincidentally, Sam's son Chris was playing football for Erewash 2012 FC which, as the name suggests, was a newly-formed Club playing in the Long Eaton Sunday League. They finished bottom of the bottom Division in their inaugural season after being soundly thrashed most weeks and they were desperately in need of someone to get them organised. Chris suggested to Richard that he needed a new hobby and the football team needed a manager and so Richard agreed to take the job on for the season 2013/14. The team's fortunes improved in leaps and bounds and they were no longer the wooden spoon guys holding the rest of the League up. The jewel in their crown came with an appearance at Grange Park on Sunday, May 1st, 2016, in the Divisional Cup Final. It was a game which they could quite easily have won but they were narrowly defeated 1 – 0 by Nags Head and Plough, who were already promoted as Divisional Champions.

Two or three key players had chosen to move on by the start of the following season and Erewash began the job of trying to rebuild their team. Something definitely seems to have changed because, as I write this on September 25th, 2018, they are second in the league table, having won 3 of their first 4 games. They are playing with more consistency and confidence but it remains to be seen what they actually achieve by the end of the season, which is the real test. The main thing is that, with results like these, they must be enjoying their football more.

On a more personal note, Richard and Sam had been partners for almost 20 years when they finally made the decision to tie the knot. They spent almost two years on the planning and, following several meetings with the local Vicar, the ceremony took place on Friday, August 7th, 2015, in the picturesque village of Mortehoe in Devon. They discovered and fell in love with this place whilst on holiday in the area some years ago and have been regular visitors since. With the help and cooperation of the Reverend Giles King-Smith, they turned what was originally a romantic dream into reality. They have continued to visit every year since and in fact, as I write this on September 27th, 2018, they are there this very week. The residents of Mortehoe, most of whom had gathered either in the church or on the street for the ceremony, have played a big part in their lives in one way or another. None more so than Reverend Giles, whose advice was invaluable and Richard and Sam now feel part of the village community. The Reverend's other claim to fame is that his late father Dick King-Smith, who was a farmer by profession, wrote the classic book "The Sheep Pig", subsequently adapted to make the film "Babe", released in 1996.

Their next move was to secure the purchase of their home, consolidating their commitment to a long-term future. As of this week, Chris and Charlotte are celebrating their first wedding anniversary, Hannah and Rob have set a provisional date in 2020 for their wedding and Charlotte and Robbie have announced their engagement whilst on holiday in San Francisco. Positive news all round and long may it continue.

By June, 1991, Carole had graduated from the uncertainty of a temporary contract to the security of a full time staff contract at DSA and she very soon established herself as a reliable and popular member of the team. She earned this reputation mainly because she was always on hand and willing to assist colleagues and also for her calm telephone manner when dealing with the often irate members of the Driving Examiners' and Instructors' Fraternity. She was also supportive of many of the out-of-hours social gatherings, especially when called to the bar at the "Tap and Tumbler". She made friends easily but there were 3 or 4 of the ladies that she particularly took a liking to, even to the point of going away on holiday trips. One of the ladies was the vivacious Audrey Williams who, at that time, was in the throes of being swept off her feet by one of her work colleagues. The two of them eventually upped sticks to his native Wales to get married and they then moved again, this time to Southampton, where they currently live with their son James. These days, communication between Carole and Audrey tends to be infrequent and is usually limited to the exchange of cards at birthdays and Christmas.

Carole also befriended Yancey Kelly but she turned out to be nothing more than a ship that passed in the night. After spending a weekend in Whitby and another week away in Weymouth, Carole didn't hear from her for weeks at a time and the friendship seemed to dissipate and I think she is resigned to that now. Carole also became friendly with Rebecca Sloane, who was a lovely person when she was sensible but, it has to be said, was not the most reliable when tempted into taking the odd drink. That could be a description of all of us? The two of them shared a two-week holiday in Cyprus in 2001 and were also in a party of 6 of the ladies who took a trip to America in March, 2005, to sample the sights and sounds of the musical Mecca of the Deep South. They flew to Atlanta, Georgia, and then travelled by coach to Tennessee, Alabama and Louisiana, where Nashville, Graceland and New Orleans are places of particular interest. Three months after Carole's visit, New Orleans was devastated by floods in the wake of Hurricane Katrina and she found the newsreel scenes quite upsetting. Places that she had so recently enjoyed visiting were now inaccessible and apparently in ruins.

Though Carole had retired in June, 2004, she continued to support some of the office social gatherings such as birthdays and retirements, as a means of keeping in touch with folks. The friendship that she forged with Grace Douglas has proved to be one of the most enduring and rewarding and she regards her as one of her best friends. Grace and husband Bill lived in Burton Joyce and their home was within yards of the main Nottingham to Lincoln railway line. Bill was originally a printer by trade but decided on a career change and studied to qualify as a chiropractor. In April, 1996, Carole and I made a business-cum-social trip to Burton Joyce, partly to spend an hour with Grace and partly to consult Bill regarding my sciatica. That was quite an unusual week – an appointment with Bill on the Monday, an appointment at DRI on the Tuesday for an MRI scan as part of my tinnitus investigation and also the sight of the "Hale Bopp" comet. I remember gazing into the evening sky as we were waiting for the bus from Burton Joyce to Nottingham and being mesmerised by this incredible phenomenon. Such a prolonged appearance over a period of 18 months is unique in the comet world and was a once-in-a-lifetime experience for most of us.

That single session with Bill cured my sciatica, the MRI scan was negative and about twelve months later Hale Bopp had disappeared from earth's naked-eye view. Bill and Grace retired in 2002 and they had planned to spend time touring Europe by Dormobile and by boat, the ultimate objective being to acquire a retirement home in Spain. Tragically, only a few weeks after their odyssey began, the dream turned into a nightmare when Bill suffered a heart attack and did not recover. Following his death, Grace continues to live in Burton Joyce and is as active as ever with her busy social diary, her love of painting and day-tripping. On the second Monday of each month, she and Carole meet in Nottingham for lunch and an afternoon chinwag with 4 or 5 of their former work colleagues. The chinwags tend to focus on holidays or medical appointments, including details of any resultant amputations, replacements, or enhancements. The two of them occasionally get together in between times for a trip to the cinema or theatre. Those places are usually pretty quiet and they can hear each other better as they chat about their most recent excursions or medical appointments.

Another of Carole's friends, who she describes these days as one of 3 "best friends" is Gail Warrener. She lived not too far from us in Sandiacre and every couple of months or so, they would turn out in support of the local amateur dramatic society productions, either at Trent College or the Duchess Theatre. They are in regular contact by telephone most weeks. The third of her "best friends" is Denise Holmes, formerly Asman, nee Halford, and their friendship goes back 60-odd years to their Grammar School days. Soon after leaving in 1963, Denise wasted no time in spreading her wings and, in March, 1965, she married Mick Asman, originally from Spondon and a joiner by trade. Mick very kindly acted as best man when Carole and I were married in 1968.

The relationship between Carole and Denise was somewhat spasmodic and after about 1980, they saw very little of each other and then, in 1994, we received the sad news that Mick had died suddenly. Unfortunately, we couldn't make it to the funeral due to a clash of dates following the recent demise of Carole's cousin Norman. A chance encounter with Denise and new partner Peter Holmes whilst on holiday in Blackpool in 1996 resulted in a natter in the street about them being on the look-out for an opportunity in the holiday accommodation business. A further 20 years elapsed before they were reunited, again by chance, when they met on a Number 15 bus en route to Ilkeston and this time they exchanged phone numbers. They have met up a few times since for coffee and a natter and the chance to reminisce and they also travelled to Skegness to relive a schooldays trip.

Carole still thinks of Audrey with great affection but contact with her these days is little more than an exchange of cards at Xmas and birthdays. Her relationship with Denise, Grace and Gail, however, is very much alive and they are in fairly regular contact. In 2007, whilst on holiday in Turkey, Rebecca became friends with Bayram, a young local man who was a member of the staff at her hotel. She'd hardly had time to catch her breath after returning home from the holiday when she decided to return to the hotel and the pair decided that they needed to be together. Following their whirlwind romance, they were married there and then and Rebecca returned home this time as Mrs Bayram Demerci and her flat in Nottingham served as their ready-made marital home. He managed to get himself a job at Pork Farms and they were very happy together. Tragically, it all came to a premature end when Rebecca became seriously ill and did not recover. She died on April 15th, 2009, aged 44, leaving Bayram devastated – we are led to believe that he still lives in the flat.

June 8th, 1968 is a significant date because that is the day that Carole and I were married. June 6th, 1944 is a significant date, internationally known as "D-Day", because this was when the evacuation of Dunkirk began. June 6th, 2006 is also a significant date because it was on that day that we acquired our first Seat Ibiza (FG 55 FYZ) to replace our Rover 100 "Kensington". We bought this car from Willoughby's Seat dealership in Beeston – it was 6 months old and had been used from new solely as a dealership courtesy car. Rather than face the hassle of trying to sell the Rover, we offered it to Hannah as a token of congratulations on passing her driving test recently. She was only too pleased to accept.

June 26th, 2006, is a significant date in this family because that is the day our grandson James William (Jim) was born. Kathryn was not in the best of form following the birth and by the time Jim was 3 months old, Carole was spending one day per week with them at Woolley Moor. That didn't last long, however, because Kathryn had cats in the house and they triggered Carole's allergy. It was decided that Sean would drop Jim off with us on Tuesday mornings on his way to work in Derby and then pick him up on his way home. This worked well for a time between about October, 2006, and the beginning of 2009, at which time Hetty had a fall at Bennett Street and needed surgery on her broken hip. Following Hetty's discharge from hospital, Carole found the daily routine of looking after her Mum and Dad was pretty much a full time job. With great reluctance, we were forced to give up Tuesdays with Jim and Sean enrolled him for an extra day at nursery. Kathryn had planned to return to work at some point but that didn't happen because she never really regained full fitness.

Over a period of months, Carole had noticed subtle changes in Hetty's behaviour and in 2009, after recovering from the hip surgery, she was diagnosed with dementia. During the following 3 months her short-term memory loss became a problem which meant that, because she was still so physically active, she now needed 24/7 supervision. Carole's Dad Jim simply wasn't well enough or mobile enough, and the ever-increasing demand on Carole's time and energy spent toing and froing between home and Bennett Street was taking its toll. 2009 had been a difficult period for everyone but none more so than Carole, who was running herself into the ground and had lost 2 stones in weight. It came as something of a relief when her Dad was admitted to hospital for a second time on December 10th, 2009. Whilst it would obviously have been preferable that he wasn't ill, at least he was now in the best place to receive the care he needed.

There was now only Hetty to look after at home and the visiting nurse suggested that it might be an opportunity for her to go into respite care for a fortnight and she would look for somewhere suitable. This would mean a change of scenery for Hetty and would also give Carole some breathing space and perhaps more time to visit her Dad. On Wednesday, December 16th, 2009, Hetty moved somewhat reluctantly into Ashmere Care Home in West Hallam, initially for a 3-week period of respite. The following day, December 17th, Carole went to the Royal Derby to visit her Dad and she arrived to find him apparently lifeless in his bed. She alerted the nurse, who'd said that she'd only just left him after popping in to turn him over but it seems that between then and Carole arriving, he'd slipped away. Jim used to say that he would be proud to reach the age of 90 but he died one week before his 89th birthday and, sadly, didn't quite make it. The funeral service took place at Bramcote Crematorium on Monday, January 4th, 2010.

CHAPTER 9

Carole and I decided that we were in a position to think about treating ourselves to a new car for the first time ever. We thought that we may not get the chance again and so we decided to trade in our Seat Ibiza in favour of a new version of the same model. We took delivery of our new Seat Ibiza 1.2 (FE 60 FLA) on September 1st, 2010 and we are still driving it, though mileage is down to about 20 miles per week. That is sufficient for my return journey to the newsagent's each morning and to Tesco for the weekly shopping, usually on Wednesdays. I get no pleasure from sharing the roads with some of the morons we come across today and, if habits and attitudes are anything to go by, I strongly suspect that many of them have never even taken a driving test, let alone passed one. Rule 1 when I started driving was "Consideration for other road users" – what the hell went wrong? Considering the volume of traffic on our roads today, I would have thought it sensible to adopt a policy of less speed, more patience, but the exact opposite seems to prevail. Help.

Hetty's 3-week respite break stretched into 3 years and then into 5 years and yet she never lost that feisty attitude which had served her so well over her lifetime and had endeared her to all of us. The average life expectancy of patients in Hetty's situation is estimated to be about 3 years and, considering that she was 90 when admitted, she was doing extraordinarily well, which was no surprise to those of us who knew her. Carole was at odds with her conscience over the situation but there really was no choice because the average family simply cannot cope with the needs of these patients. Carole got into a routine of visiting two or three times a week for the duration, even when Hetty had to be hospitalised on a couple of occasions, the last occasion being June 14th, 2017, following another fall, this time at the care home. She had surgery within 24 hours to repair her broken left femur and after one week's R & R, she was discharged on June 21st and returned to West Hallam.

It wasn't long before problems began to develop, the most serious being the loss of the ability to swallow which meant, of course, that she was unable to eat or drink properly. By the middle of July, her health had deteriorated to such a degree that it was now only a matter of time. Carole was determined that there would not be a repeat of events when she arrived just too late to be with her Dad in his final minutes and each day from July 16th, she kept a 10-hour vigil at the home. The staff took it in turns to stop by Hetty's room to see how they were doing and so they weren't short of company or refreshments during those final days. Inevitably, Hetty's now-frail form finally succumbed and she died on Wednesday, July 19th, 2017, at 18:30, two days before her 99th birthday. The funeral took place at Bramcote Crematorium on August 8th, 2017, the service being conducted by the Reverend Geoffrey Halliday. The eulogy was recounted by Carole's cousin Brian Clifton in a fitting tribute to a well-loved and respected lady, now reunited with Jim, her husband of 66 years.

Six years had passed since I'd given up playing golf and I'd become bored with the routine that I'd got into of twice-daily social visits to the Club and I was ready for a change. I needed something new to occupy my time and I thought I'd follow Richard's lead and try my hand at writing. This idea was born mainly out of a desire to leave something behind when I'm gone as a bit of a legacy that folks might care to read. I thought that might be a change from the time-honoured tradition of wading through the old photos, most of which I'm not on anyway. Dad was a gifted writer with a beautiful hand but the only examples I have of that are two letters which he wrote to his sister Mag and the first three pages of his version of "Memory Lane", which he had typed. He had moved to Plymouth in May, 1969, and these three documents were written during the last 6 months of his life whilst he was working the nightshift at Bush. They are of sentimental value to me, not necessarily because of their content but because he had a knack of writing it the way he spoke it.
I didn't really know what I wanted to write about but I picked up my pen and pad and started with a couple of essays of about 1,000 words which were mostly nonsense. I came across an article in the Times newspaper in which Lord Coe was attempting to describe his contribution towards the changing of the rules and procedures which govern false starts in athletics events. Oh, joy! I was somewhat puzzled by what I read and decided that I would write to him for clarification but first, I needed some proper writing equipment in preference to using green crayon. An electric typewriter was a priority but finding one, either used or new, was easier said than done. Eventually, in April, 2011, Carole happened to spot one

in a charity shop and she paid £10 for it. It seemed to be functional and so, paper and carbon to hand, I dared to write to Lord Coe on September 10th, 2011, but, for reasons unknown, I didn't get a reply.

I hadn't used a typewriter in 20-odd years, since my Riverside days in fact, so I made a start by typing up the bits and bobs which I'd previously hand-written. Not only would this be good practice but these documents, though I didn't know it at the time, were the start of my filing system, which has swelled to about 150 documents over the last 10 years. I liked the machine but it soon developed problems with the ribbon and we couldn't get a replacement until a friend came across a source on the internet. It was claimed that the ribbons were genuine and suitable for our model but we couldn't get them to fit properly and so it was bye-bye typewriter.

My writing career was seemingly over before it had begun but then Sean and Carole arrived home from Chesterfield on May 11th, 2013, carrying this very laptop, together with accompanying printer and paper. Sean set everything up and I was now ready, willing and able to communicate with anyone who I thought might be in need of some advice. The learning curve, however, was quite steep for a PC novice like me and I began to doubt that I'd ever get the hang of the stupid thing. I eventually learned a degree of self-control and was able to discipline myself sufficiently to think rather than curse when things went awry. I now feel reasonably confident with some of the basics, though I don't profess to understand them, and if I stay in my comfort zone and rely on the odd fluke, I can produce a reasonable letter. After spending the first 3 months falling out, when words such as "bin" and "hammer" were frequently overheard, I have learnt to stay reasonably calm and the machine has learnt to reasonably behave itself and we now rub along OK.

Since February, 2014, I have had a total of about 30 letters published in the local papers, 17 of those in the Derby Telegraph. I am extremely proud of the fact that 3 of those contributions won the coveted "Letter of the Week" award. Whilst it is always a bit of a thrill to see our efforts appear on the letters pages, I admit to having become somewhat disillusioned with the idea of late. For me, it is a means of making readers aware of my views and when I consistently fail to stimulate a response of any kind, supportive or otherwise, whatever the issue, it all seems rather pointless. Since acquiring the laptop, I have come to appreciate the time it must have taken for some clever people to develop this ingenious piece of kit which, in my case, was initially bought merely to replace a defunct typewriter. I have spent countless hours at this keyboard composing letters and essays but this current assignment, which has hitherto taken about 6 years, on and off, is by far the grandest that I have yet undertaken.

I've barely begun to scratch the surface when it comes to the laptop's capabilities but one of these days maybe I'll get around to exploring it further and create something fancy. Contrary to modern trends, I had always been content to manage my life without the need for a computer or mobile phone, and I'd never felt the urge to get involved with either. Suddenly in 2013, this laptop came into my life and opened up a whole new world for me, which now includes WIFI connection to the internet, to boot. By August, 2015, I had made the decision to equip myself with a mobile phone in order to be in the loop with everyone else in that regard as well. I'm not that keen on phone calls and much prefer to communicate by text message as it is far more relaxed and less invasive.

It was during the month of December, 2018, that I happened to be browsing on t'internet whilst taking a break from writing. I decided to look up some old friends from Erewash Valley GC and my first target was Mike Ronan. There was a mobile number listed on the site and with some trepidation, I decided to send a text message. I wasn't sure what to expect as my last contact with Mike was in 1993 when I visited him at Erewash to buy clubs for Sean. His response to my message was prompt and cordial and he suggested that we meet up for tea and toast (with jam), just like the old days. We thought that Trent Lock GC might be a suitable venue but, after exchanging several messages, we decided to delay our meeting until the New Year, 2019. It made sense because his wife Margaret had not been well and I wasn't feeling at my best either.

For several weeks I'd been having difficulty dropping off to sleep at night and quite often I would be back downstairs within minutes of going to bed. It was almost as if I was afraid to go to sleep in case I stopped breathing, though why this should be, I hadn't the faintest idea. Every time I sat down I was nodding off, things were dropping from my grasp and I couldn't finish my meals because I was falling asleep over them. By Christmas, 2018, things had got worse to the point where I was hallucinating and not making a lot of sense – this sometimes happens when the brain is starved of oxygen, apparently. I was convinced that our next-door neighbours were laying a carpet in their lounge in the middle of the night and there was a man and a woman sitting outside on our patio chatting. I had also seen a mouse in the bedroom and a shrouded figure lying across the bed waiting to get a clear shot at it with a crossbow! Looking back, the covered figure that I'd seen in the bedroom must have been the turned-back duvet but as for the mouse, the carpet-laying and the chatting couple, I've no idea.

By now, Carole was adamant that I should see a doctor and she called Breaston surgery on the morning of Wednesday, January 3rd, 2019, to request a home visit. A lady doctor, a stranger, arrived at about midday and after giving me the once-over, she said that my blood-sugar and blood-oxygen levels were low. She called the surgery for advice and they were adamant that I should go into hospital, the thought of which didn't appeal to me one bit.

I remember an ambulance arriving and two lady paramedics getting me into a wheelchair and then I must have fallen asleep because I cannot recall being loaded into the ambulance or the "blue light and siren" journey to the Royal Derby Hospital. My first recollection was when I was being woken by Nurse Pam at 07:30 the following morning (Thursday) and being told that I was in the High Dependency Unit (HDU) on Ward 403. I had been "out of it" for about 18 hours and have no recollection of my admission at all but, because of the state I was in, Carole had apparently been warned to prepare for the worst. Over time, due to my respiratory rate dropping whilst I was sleeping, my blood-oxygen had gradually dropped to a dangerously low level. The immediate priority was to expel the carbon dioxide which had replaced the oxygen in my blood and replace that with oxygen. This is a slow process which involves using a clip-on nasal oxygen supply by day and the wearing of a mask connected to a small bedside ventilator by night. The ventilator (NIV) ensures that my respiratory rate is maintained should it falter whilst I'm asleep. For numerous reasons, there is no guarantee that this therapy will work for all patients but it is the best option available at this time. Thankfully, it worked for me and I'm still here to tell the tale.

After spending 3 nights in HDU my stats had improved sufficiently so that I could be moved along the corridor to spend a couple of nights on my own in one of the side rooms. From there I was moved again to share a ward with 3 other chaps, one of whom was coughing up blood now and again and he wasn't well at all. Another was "Bert" who, despite a lung problem, managed to make his way to the kiosk each morning to collect our newspapers. Senior Consultant Dr John Anderson usually led the daily tour of the Ward on Monday, Wednesday and Friday mornings, accompanied by his entourage of colleagues. He would chat briefly and, having collated the latest data, update us on our progress, discuss any concerns and explain the next stage of our treatment.

The nursing staff appeared regularly throughout the day to check vitals, i.e. blood pressure, heart rate, oxygen, etc., to administer medication and to take blood samples. Our physios, often two ladies in tandem, would call in to check on our progress with a view to getting us up and about at the earliest opportunity. It is they who give us the final once-over prior to being discharged and their test takes about 5 minutes. It involves negotiating a flight of 10 stairs up and down reasonably safely and the only way to fail is if we go headlong from top to bottom. Should that happen, we then "pick ourselves up, dust ourselves down and start all over again".

The normal blood-oxygen level should be between 95% and 99% and the target range for my oxygen level, which I believe was below 80% when I was admitted, had been set initially at 88–92%, which I think was achieved after 4 or 5 days. Once the target was reached, we began the process of gradually reducing the oxygen supply rate each day. The oxygen supply was very gentle, even on the initial setting of 2 (litres-per-minute) and as my levels improved, it was gradually reduced to 1.5, 1.0 and 0.5 and barely noticeable. After a week or so, it was turned off altogether and I was monitored to check that my blood-oxygen level remained stable. By Friday morning (January 11th), Dr John brought the welcome news that I had made excellent progress and, depending on the result of one more blood test, as far as he was concerned I was "MFFD"

(Medically Fit for Discharge). I would then need to pass the Physio test before my discharge papers could be signed.

He had hinted on Wednesday that I may be able to go home on Friday and that now seemed to be confirmed. I had the blood test and didn't hear any more on that so I presume it must have been satisfactory and by mid-afternoon I had been given the all-clear by the Physios. We were now waiting for Pharmacy to dispense my medication but unfortunately there was a delay on that as one of the items had to be delivered by courier and the 4-hour wait seemed like an eternity. It was 20:15 by the time the Head of Pharmacy arrived on the Ward with my bag of stuff and apologies and she left Sister to explain all while she went to order the taxi for my journey home. Staff Nurse Ron gave me a steady wheelchair ride down to the car park (mostly in the lift), Abdul gave me a steady ride home along the A52 in his gleaming Mercedes and I eventually landed at 21:00. In the words of the song: "It's very nice to go trav'ling, but it's so much nicer to come home" and there's no place on earth that's cosier than your own bed. I really don't know how to thank the Team who sorted me out so effectively but I hope that I am never in need of their expertise again.

CHAPTER 10

And so to the spring of 2019 and some research into my former Erewash GC golfing companion Eamonn Darcy told me that he played his last tournament in December, 2018, and had now retired from the professional circuit. His career spanned 50 years, with the last 15 having been spent on the European Seniors Tour and the US Champions' Tour. The pinnacle of his career must have been when he was selected to play in the Ryder Cup on no less than four occasions. His achievements in the game established him as one of Ireland's greatest-ever players. All this got me thinking about the early days in his career when I first met him at Erewash Valley GC in the mid-1970s. He and his wife Suzanne now live on a 35-acre property in Enniskerry, County Wicklow, which is about 6 miles south of Dublin and 5 miles from the village of Delgany, where he was born. From the description of this place, it is a smallholding which is within 5 miles of the Irish Sea coast and within 5 miles of the Wicklow Mountains to the west. I got the impression that if there ever was such a place as "God's Little Acre", he was now living there.

I was curious to know whether he would remember those early days at Erewash and so I decided to cobble together an address and wrote to him in April, 2019. We are now midway through 2022 and I am beginning to think that I won't be getting a reply, despite Richard exchanging e-mails with his agent at one point. I cannot imagine that my letter could have failed to arrive in Dublin on the mail plane, or that the local Postie in Enniskerry wouldn't be aware that Eamonn was living on his patch. It is disappointing when folks are apparently far too busy to acknowledge correspondence or can't bring themselves to recall their humble beginnings. A simple "hello, how are you doing?" would suffice, even if he can't remember who the hell I am. Such a small gesture costs nothing and can mean a lot to us ordinary folks but I suppose it's down to a question of manners and sparing five minutes of his valuable time to send a text message.

Moving forward to July, 2019, I had read in the Derby Telegraph that long-time friend Roger Smith had compiled a history of the Derby music scene as it was during the 1960's. Aptly titled "When the Stars Came into Town", it's the story of Derby's main entertainment venues, the star names who frequented them and the fans who supported them during those vibrant years. I sent him my congratulations and he agreed to my suggestion that we should swap signed copies of the fruits of our labours. He said that he would let Doug know that I'd been in touch and I didn't have to wait long for Doug's response and the outcome of our chat was that we arranged to meet at the Pip Tree Café, Collyer's Nursery, Borrowash, on Monday, July 22nd, 2019, at 10:00. Carole and I are certain that it was a Monday and fairly sure that it was July 22nd, though I don't have any written record of the actual date. This was due to the fact that between December, 2018 and April, 2021, I didn't keep a diary and my notebook entries are not always dated. I have since come to realise how important it is to date stuff, even the scribble – it can be a great help. Carole, myself and Doug arrived at Collyer's car park safely and punctually, only to find that the stupid Pip Tree sodding Café doesn't open on Mondays. Never mind, we said, let's venture into the village and look for somewhere else.

The Caffe Torta (formerly the Noah's Ark pub) on Nottingham Road was the lucky venue and, with more staff than customers, it was quiet and proved ideal for our two-hour chat. Doug had thought to bring his laptop along loaded with memorabilia and photos of the old days, some familiar but some which Carole and I were seeing for the first time. Health issues inevitably came into the conversation and at that time Doug was undergoing a course of treatment on his troublesome throat. He was a bit miffed that he had been advised, at least for the time being, to take a break from the vocals with "Godfrey's Grit & Soul". This was a grand way to spend a morning before going our separate ways at 13:00, with a pledge to meet up again soon.

I remember cricket being played on the meadow at the end of Kimberley Road when I was a nipper. This was between 1950 and 1956 and I just took it for granted that the team I used to watch was Borrowash CC. Dad was involved with this team in several guises – groundsman, occasional umpire and occasional player were a few and whenever he was on duty, in whatever capacity, I wasn't far away. From the age of about two when I could just about stand and totter, his passion for the game had already begun to rub off on me and I can't recall a time when it hasn't been a part of my life, if only in sentiment. There were plans to extend and redevelop Kimberley Road and those balmy days of cricket on our meadow were numbered, the last match being played there in August, 1956. Borrowash CC had now lost their ground and, as there was no alternative site within the village, the team was facing disbandment. Thankfully, the day was saved when homeless Borrowash CC amalgamated with Ockbrook CC, thus giving rise to the Ockbrook and Borrowash CC (O&BCC) that we are familiar with today.

Plausible though it may sound, the amalgamation part of this story is no more than a figment of my imagination and there is no truth in it whatsoever. I was too young to think about making any enquiries of any sort at the time but I had imagined that this was how events unfolded. After all, it seemed a completely natural and obvious way to solve the problems that Borrowash CC were facing. For the next 60 years, or so, I never had any reason to question my erroneous conclusions until 2019 when I tried to do some research into Borrowash cricket with a view to writing about it. My search for info on t'internet yielded virtually nothing and it was only now that I began to discover the truth.

There was no doubt at all that I'd watched cricket in Borrowash as a youngster but one dead end led to another. I was on the point of giving up when, out of sheer frustration, I decided to contact a former school mate. The Wheatleys were neighbours of ours on Kimberley Road and their younger son Roy and I went through school together from infants' to O-levels, after which time, I left. We've had only fleeting contact since those days but I decided to give it a whirl. As far as I knew, Roy wasn't at all sport-orientated and he had no recollection of cricket being played at Kimberley Road but his wife's father and brother had been associated with O&BCC. This sounded promising but when Roy asked them about Borrowash cricket, they seemed to have difficulty in making any useful contribution at all – another dead end. Roy happened to mention my quest to Anton Rippon, the former sports writer at the Derby Telegraph, and he suggested that I get in touch with O&BCC as any such merger would almost certainly have been entered in their records.

It was during September, 2019 that I decide to call O&BCC and spoke to Madam Secretary Jane Hough. She was adamant that, to the best of her knowledge, there had been no merger with anyone or change of name since the Club was first formed in 1850. She also said, in her forthright manner, that she wasn't even aware that Borrowash ever had a cricket team. Jane's candid reaction to my enquiry left me in no doubt that my fairy story had now been comprehensively blown out of the water. She did, however, take the opportunity to remind me that The Derbyshire Cricket League, founded in 1919, was currently in the midst of its Centenary celebrations and a special commemorative yearbook was on sale at all Member Clubs. Carole and I had no hesitation in making the trip to Ockbrook to collect our copy – my first visit to the ground since I was about 15-years-old.

The burning question now was, if the team that I used to watch on Kimberley Road meadow wasn't Borrowash CC, then who were they? I was stumped once again and, with the inexorable passage of time, I assumed that anyone who may have any information would now be scattered far and wide, or no longer with us. I had run out of ideas regarding who might be able to help when, in a flash of inspiration, my brother Ken sprang to mind. He was living at home with us until National Service beckoned in 1952 – I called him. He, like Roy, had very little obvious interest in sport and so had paid little heed to the cricket but he had no hesitation in confirming that Borrowash never had a cricket team and the mystery team was in fact Borrowash Wesleyan Methodist Youth Club XI. He had grown up with all the lads who played for the team and was aware of their activities, if not particularly interested. Thanks Ken – we have lift-off.

I felt that I now had some positive and reliable info on which to base my story of Borrowash cricket, even if it was only the fact that Borrowash never had a cricket team! Of the players who turned out for the Youth Club team, I recalled the names RAB (Tony) Burrows, Brian Moore and Ray Stokes, all of which were indelibly etched in my memory, though I'm not sure why. There were other names and faces on the misty periphery of my memory but none was as prominent as those three, though I can't recall ever having spoken to any of them, or them to me. I had read in the Derby Telegraph quite recently that Brian had died and was therefore eliminated from my search of the local phone directories. No lead with RAB Burrows but there was a Stokes, R, listed at a Draycott address, which seemed promising and so, after taking a few deep breaths, I dialled the number. I found to my astonishment that I was actually speaking to the man himself for the very first time. "Raymond Stokes speaking – how may I help you?" he said. Bullseye – I couldn't believe it. When I explained who I was and the reason for the call, he seemed quite flattered that someone should be taking such an interest in the team after so long and offered to help in any way he could.

I mailed him a questionnaire, which he completed and returned and, without any prompting, he was thoughtful enough to enclose a copy of a photo of the team. It was taken in 1950 and Ray had kindly written the names of those featured on the back. That photo, though by no means rare, reflects a bygone age which is so dear to me and I shall treasure it always. I think Ray probably had the most authoritative voice I'd ever heard and, even at the age of 89, he said that his memories of those days were still so vivid. He remembered Dad, describing him as "Edgar, the best groundsman around – he worked wonders with that field and the square". The cricket at Kimberley Road finally came to an end and, sadly, the team had little choice but to disband. The lads who were still keen on playing joined other clubs and, ironically, Ray himself initially signed for O&BCC and subsequently for Draycott CC before eventually hanging up his bat. He still meets Arthur "Nip" Anderton regularly for a pint.

I spent about a month writing what was initially intended to be a labour of love but I have to admit that I found it hard work. Had it not been for Ray's interest, I may not have finished it because it seemed to be short on story and long on padding. It had, however, served to get the monkey off my back in revealing the true story of Borrowash cricket, which was the point of the exercise really, and that made it worthwhile. I was told that there are no surviving records of the team's exploits during those 6 years, much to my disappointment. I suspect that any such memorabilia was probably kept under lock and key by Frank Smith and lost forever after his death in 1969. Truly heartbreaking – I would pay a king's ransom to be able to browse through one of the scorebooks. I sent the completed document to Ray by recorded delivery, rather than deliver it in person, in the middle of December, 2019.

Three or four weeks passed and we were now into the middle of January, 2020. I'd heard nothing from Ray and so decided to call him but there was no answer, which seemed odd – perhaps he's gone away, I thought. I waited a further week and called again and this time I got a continuous beep, which suggested that the line had been disconnected. I was now rather concerned and began to wonder if something had happened to him? Ray had mentioned that he was still in touch with Arthur Anderton and so, because I was so concerned about the situation, I reluctantly decided to call Arthur. He told me that Ray had moved house and was now living in Oakwood but he didn't have his phone number or address, which I thought was rather odd. There were pauses in the conversation and he seemed reluctant to say anything unless prompted but he gave me his assurance that he'd let me have Ray's contact details, as and when. He seemed uneasy, as though I was an intruder trying to steal something from him and it occurred to me that he'd been told to keep shtoom regarding Ray's move. It comes as no surprise that I've not heard from either of them since – it seemed as though I'd been dropped, like the proverbial "hot potato". Why that should be, I don't know, but I shall always wonder whether Ray ever read my essay.

I don't remember having any contact with my brother Ken after Aunty Mag's funeral on March 25th, 2010, until I called him in September, 2019 about my cricket story. During September/October, 2019, I called him on 3 or 4 Sunday mornings just for a chat and he said that he'd like to read the story when it was finished. He said that he'd got problems with his chest and had been undergoing tests at the hospital and their diagnosis confirmed mesothelioma and there was nothing that could be done. Having been out of touch for almost 10 years, I had no idea that he was even ill but the reality was that he was now living on borrowed time. Obviously, he was in some distress and had difficulty trying to talk about it. He died on December 7th, 2019, about two weeks before I'd finished my story.

On May 20th, 2020, Carole had a fall in the kitchen which resulted in a trip to the hospital with a broken right humerus. Subsequent tests revealed signs of osteoporosis, more commonly known as "brittle bones", for which she was prescribed medication and dietary advice. She very soon developed a nuisance cough which the hospital said could be attributed to this particular medication but despite changing it, the cough persisted. As an alternative treatment, they suggested "osteoporosis infusion" and she went to the Royal Derby for the first stage of the procedure on October 4th, 2022. It takes about two hours and has to be administered once a year for three years, by which time we hope that the cough may be cured.

At the beginning of March, 2020, Prime Minister Boris Johnson embarked on a series of live appearances on TV. Initially, the purpose of these appearances was to deliver warning to the nation that coronavirus (COVID) was making deadly progress through Europe and it was inevitable that it would soon arrive on our shores. It was growing into pandemic proportions and he feared that many lives would be lost, he said. He appeared regularly each day at 17:00 to deliver these live TV bulletins, which were little more than a procession of gloom and doom platitudes, delivered in his best Churchillian style for added effect. For the next 2½ years, this government subjected us to a mishmash of u-turns, delayed and wrong decisions, guesses and patronising garbage. Because of my medical condition, I was officially listed as a "vulnerable person" and as such, received advice bulletins from the then Health Secretary, Matt Hancock. These were addressed to "Dear Stephen" and signed "Matt". Such familiarity is neither appropriate nor appreciated and I doubt that he is qualified to give worthwhile advice to anyone about anything.

If the atmosphere emanating from Downing Street wasn't deliberately designed to create insecurity that is most certainly what it unwittingly achieved. We were made to feel that we should be totally reliant on this government to protect us, to show us the way forward and to lead us to salvation. Should we really be eternally grateful to this government for taking such difficult decisions in the interests of our well-being? What they had actually achieved was to deliberately create confusion at every opportunity in order to undermine public confidence and morale to such a degree that none of us would be sure of anything anymore. We were treated as though we needed protection from ourselves as it was highly likely that some of us would try to make a reckless bid for freedom and deliberately try to become infected by this deadly virus. We were cowering in our homes, afraid to venture out, awaiting the next instalment of their off-the-cuff "strategy", details of which "would be announced next Tuesday" by some nobody whose turn it was to face the cameras. If we'd been allowed to use common sense and left to our own devices from the outset, we would never have been in such a pathetic state.

The propaganda in these TV bulletins was originally proffered as "guidance" but very soon became "rules" and quickly escalated to "laws". Our freedom and rights became so restricted and abandoned that any transgressors, none of whom had actually committed any crime, were regarded as "lawbreakers". They were arrested, assaulted, manhandled, labelled as criminals, beaten, fined, threatened with jail, with a record for life – and that was just the ladies. Newly-recruited "police officers" were conscripted specifically for the purpose of bullying and assaulting members of the public whose only "crime" was to merely exercise their legal rights. These "policemen" were akin to the jailbirds and thugs who were assigned to special duties in the film "The Dirty Dozen" – offered a penal deal for doing the government's dirty work. I think this is known as "conditioning", a means of bringing us to heel and training us to "sit" on command. Some of us are sick and tired of being dictated to by this gang of smart-arsed, useless schoolkids who dare to call themselves a "government". We are denied any voice or appeal – is this all we have to vote for?

It is worth noting that, within a 3-week period during January, 2020, there were 8,000 cases of coronavirus recorded globally, spread over four continents – Asia, Australasia, South America and North America. In my view, this virus did not escape but was transported and it seems likely that the current 7 million "with covid" deaths recorded globally are neither unfortunate nor accidental. From the very outset, this government assumed total control of every aspect of this saga and the Prime Minister has achieved a remarkable success rate in his predictions – how does he do it? The Gypsy Petulengro, who plys her fortune-telling trade from a kiosk on Central Pier in Blackpool, might do well to seek his advice. In the last 3½ years, approximately 230,000 "with covid" deaths have been recorded in England alone and it's highly likely that there will be a few more yet. This is despite the "best efforts" of this government in trying to deal with the situation.

What gives this Prime Minister the right to delay a public enquiry until what he considers to be "an appropriate time"? This stalling is the direct result, yet again, of meddling and manipulation by this man because he knows full well that the longer the delay, the more clouded memories become and the greater the risk of the onset of apathy. This ploy is as old as the hills and is typical of Johnson and yet we meekly accept it – something else he's been allowed to get away with. Mercifully, after almost 3 pointless years in office, he finally succumbed to the inevitable when he resigned on July 7th, 2022. By the end of June, 2022, despite repeated reminders from him of what his government has achieved during the covid pandemic, the fact is that official statistics told us that there were 250,000 "with covid" deaths in the UK in just over 3½ years. In the beginning, the goalposts were moved so often with regard to the way that these deaths were identified and calculated until, eventually, a system that doesn't necessarily reveal the truth was approved. The true figure is anybody's guess and, in reality, it is likely to be a lot higher than the official statistics tell us. The psychological damage has been done and the regularity of new covid outbreaks ensures that we spend our lives living under this perpetual cloud.

Any gambler would surely be skint and suicidal following a run of bad luck such as we have endured over the past 3½ years. Never in the field of human conflict have we had covid, Brexit, fuel and energy prices through the roof, inflation at a 40-year high, war in Europe, strikes, monkeypox, heatwaves, floods, polio, wildfires, drought, lockdowns and blackouts, all within the space of 3 years. If that isn't enough, we have a Prime Minister who is too crass and too arrogant to take advice and he has no concept of reality. He believes that forever swimming against the tide is the mark of good leadership and courage. In fact, it simply causes confrontation and delay, makes hard work of everything and avoids solutions, which is the modus operandi in Westminster. It ensures that everything is "on-going", nothing is ever achieved or solved and we only go backwards, as we have for the last 50 years, and these highly-paid, useless Hooray-Henrys are never out of a job.

The first rule in Westminster is that if a department is working well, reorganise or dismantle it and if it isn't working well, ignore it. His cynical attitude has finally tightened the last screw in the coffin of our once-lauded Democracy. Whenever he is challenged, he is evasive and less than truthful and seems to take pride in publicly flaunting his disrespect for the rule of law which governs a civilised society. He displays all the traits of a spoilt, rebellious child. We are left to wonder what they have in store for us next – haven't we suffered enough? "We promise not to do it again, Lord, whatever in the hell it was we did" – Cable Hogue in the 1970 film.

CHAPTER 11

During the mid-summer weeks of 2020 our patio evening primroses served as a feeding station for three elephant hawkmoth caterpillars. Carole discovered one whilst weeding and tidying up the patio and, not being sure of what it was other than a caterpillar, she moved it into the garden. She'd hardly done that when we spotted two more of these extraordinary creatures munching on the primrose leaves. They are quite startling at first sight simply because of their size, roughly that of a man's index finger. They spent the month of September systematically stripping the plants of their leaves until, having had their fill and become sufficiently mature, they made their way down to the ground. We watched as they made their way across the patio, only to disappear into the undergrowth, where they would spend the winter months pupating. All being well, they will emerge as adult moths between May and July next year and, during their short life span of only 5 weeks on the wing, they will find a mate and the cycle will begin all over again. We'd never seen anything quite like these fascinating creatures before and we've not seen anything like them since – another first.

By the middle of June, 2020, some 18 months after first being hospitalised with hypercapnia, I was struggling again with similar symptoms so we decided to buy a pulse oximeter. This is a matchbox-sized gadget which gently clamps on to any middle digit and the display reveals blood-oxygen level and heart rate. This we did within a couple of days and my blood-oxygen was indeed low, which suggested that I was heading down the same road, though not yet hallucinating. By breakfast time on Friday, July 3rd, I was struggling and so Carole rang 111. An ambulance duly arrived crewed by two young men, one of whom was a trainee doctor. After checking my vitals they eventually decided that I should go into hospital. On this occasion I was conscious and recall being loaded into the ambulance and spending the journey to the Royal Derby chatting about musical preferences.

I recall parts of the examination when I was admitted, which included a doctor from "Red Team" having some difficulty obtaining a blood sample from the top of my left wrist and also a routine test for covid. Eventually, I was trollied to a waiting area before being transferred to

Room 7 on Ward 403, a single-bed, en suite side room (no HDU this time). It was now around midday and almost from the moment I arrived, the staff were buzzing around performing their various tasks. The catering lady, who I recognised from my previous visit, appeared at the door to ask if I wanted anything to eat and what would I like for tea? While one nurse was clipping an oxygen supply tube to my nose and sorting out the mask ready for bedtime, another brought in clean linen and made up the bed.

There was a constant hubbub of activity throughout most of the day – no sooner did one visitor leave than another arrived. Several times a day a nurse would arrive to wheel the mobile monitor to the bedside to check blood pressure, heart rate and oxygen level. There were some quiet interludes such as mealtimes, for example, but that wasn't guaranteed if a blood sample was needed. The 45 minutes leading up to shift changeover at 19:30 and 07:30 was probably the quietest period. Staff just seemed to vanish to update their shift reports whilst perhaps hoping that there wouldn't be any last-minute hiccup which might delay their departure at the end of a twelve-hour shift.

Over that first weekend I managed to connect some names to faces amongst the ladies – Staff Nurse Alex, who had a local accent, Nurse Pristine who I think was French, and Mary from Derby, who appeared on most days to dust round and keep the place clean and tidy. I can't recall meeting any of them on my first visit but we were on first-name terms almost from the word go. Charge Nurse Ron, who worked the night shift, was on the Team on my first visit and gave me my wheelchair ride down to the car park, if you remember? He's been at the Royal Derby for 20-odd years and is a safe pair of hands. Of the dozen or so faces I saw most often, Pristine was probably the most frequent visitor and she always had time to listen and explain stuff and also kept her ear to the ground. Michelle was our Clinical Coordinator and she was always on hand to monitor new admissions and departures. She also accompanied the doctors on their rounds to note and action any changes to medication, equipment, etc.

There are no doctors' rounds at weekends and so it wasn't until the Monday morning that I met the Team, led by Senior Consultant Dr John

Anderson once again. He led the Team that looked after me on my first visit but this time it was Dr Deepak Subramanian, who I think is of Sri Lankan origin, who I saw most often. He came in to see me pretty well every morning and I found him to be very approachable and informative and, from our first meeting, he insisted that I should call him Deepak – "it's easier". He seemed to focus mainly on the issue of COPD (Chronic Obstructive Pulmonary Disease) and said that he would like me to go for a lung scan, which I did on the Tuesday morning. In view of the fact that I had been a long-term smoker, he seemed pleasantly surprised that my lungs were in such good nick "apart from the odd bits and pieces". From my point of view, the important thing was that the scan didn't show up anything sinister and that was obviously a relief. I imagine that lung scans all too often reveal things of a more serious and depressing nature and so this result was an early bonus.

At that particular time, we were about 3 months into the covid business, having already been through the first of the lockdowns, and all hospital visiting was suspended. Even though the days were busy, they seemed long and the nights even longer due to the difficulty I had in getting to sleep on that bloody zig-zag stupid bed! The mask was akin to a medieval instrument of torture which I, like most folks I should think, found uncomfortable, if necessary. I asked if someone would come to get me into bed at about 22:00, fit the mask and connect me up and then come back at about 03:00 to release me, please. I could then sit on the side of the bed and picnic on the couple of biscuits I had saved and a glass of water before getting myself back into bed to try to nod off for a couple of hours, usually unsuccessfully. I wasn't allowed out of bed unsupervised until the two Physio ladies were happy that I was OK using the Zimmer frame. I think it was Tuesday morning when I passed that test and that meant I was able to get to the en suite toilet/shower room under my own steam and could dispense with the papier mache wee bottles. The view of the busy Uttoxeter Road from the north-facing window of my Level-4 room provided a welcome diversion. We seemed to be making progress.

The days went by and my condition steadily improved and the oxygen supply had been gradually reduced in ½ ltr increments from the 2 ltr/min starting rate and by the second weekend, it was down to ½ ltr/min and I was maintaining my oxygen levels. On Friday, July 12th, a young lady arrived with a trolley-load of stuff, to carry out a "lung capacity assessment", she said. I did the huffing and puffing into a tube while she worked the machinery. A couple of days later, another young lady arrived carrying a holdall which contained a "non-invasive ventilation kit" (NIV) which had been calibrated specially for me and was now ready for me to take home (on loan). She showed me all the bits and bobs, explaining what was what and how to assemble it all and how to fit the mask. When all that had gone in one ear and out of the other, there were instructions included and so I was quite confident that Carole and I would manage. If not, there was also a help-line number to call, should we get stuck. I now realised that the purpose of the lung test was to provide the data in order to calibrate the NIV machine to suit my lung capacity.

It was just before 18:00 on the Sunday (July 12th), I'd had my tea and Carole and I had exchanged our daily text messages as usual when Pristine appeared. I was in the armchair on one side of the bed and she was fiddling around on the other side when she asked if my oxygen was switched on? It was hardly noticeable if it was and I couldn't be sure and she then said that it was definitely off because she'd turned it off at 17:00! For the last hour, she'd been keeping a sneaky eye on me to make sure that I hadn't collapsed in a heap – I had no idea, the crafty little madam. She then walked around the bed and said, in a whisper, that she thought that I might be going home tomorrow?

Tomorrow was soon upon us and I was hoping that Pristine was right and I'd be going home today, at some stage. The doctors' rounds usually started at around 10:00 following their 09:00 prep meeting so I would know sometime between then and 12 noon, depending on which end of the Ward they started. They eventually arrived and Dr Deepak was accompanied by Dr John for only the second time on this visit so it seemed that something was afoot. He was happy with the progress I'd made to the point where I may be going home today or tomorrow but he wasn't going to rush things at this stage because he didn't want to see me back on his Ward for a third time. He said that he would like me to go down for a scan on my lower legs to make sure there were no blood clots but someone from the vascular department would be along to do a preliminary check.

The circulation in my lower legs hadn't been too clever and that gave rise to a condition known as venous exzema – the skin on my shins was dying and just flaking off. If the vascular nurse was happy then I wouldn't need the scan and that would just leave the blood test and the Physios between me and discharge. We didn't manage to fit all that in on the Monday so I was resigned to spending my eleventh night on that bloody bed. Dr John had said that I would probably be invited to attend the outpatients' Clinic in a few weeks but that didn't happen because of the covid restrictions. Telephone appointments were introduced instead.

Tuesday morning, July 14th, saw the vascular nurse arrive to give my legs the once-over with her pocket scanner and she could find no evidence of clotting. She explained that the arterial circulation to my feet was fine but it was likely that the non-return valves in the veins were weak and not working properly. The oxygen-deprived blood was leaking backwards in between heartbeats and forming pools and this meant extra work for the heart as it tried to keep the blood moving against gravity. She recommended that I wear compression stockings to help alleviate the problem and would contact my local district nurse with regard to supply. Later, the phlebotomist arrived to take a blood sample from my earlobe, the Physios turned up to put me through my paces on the stairs and Pharmacy delivered my bagful of drugs – all this in a single morning!

Pristine had said that she wanted to see me before I left but she was missing when Michelle came in on the stroke of midday to tell me that Hazel the porter was on her way to wheel me down to the departure lounge. It was about 13:00 by the time Hazel got me downstairs with my baggage, parking me up alongside the others who were waiting for transport. Idris, our volunteer driver, finally collected me at about 14:00 to wheel me across the car park to his shiny new NHS minibus for the journey home in the company of a lady from Sawley. I finally arrived home safe and sound at 15:00 on July 14th, 2020.

Dr Deepak and the Team had left no stone unturned this time in a far more thorough investigation and, for me, the trump card has to be the NIV. My problems arose initially because my respiratory rate was dropping whilst I was sleeping and my blood-oxygen level was becoming increasingly depleted and not being restored sufficiently during the day.

I had no idea that this was going on until I actually became ill but, hopefully, that issue has now been addressed and solved by the NIV therapy. The unit itself is about the size of a shoebox and virtually silent during operation and it sits unobtrusively on the bedside cabinet. The mask is far more comfortable than the one I had to wear on the Ward and I'm hardly aware of it. After we'd set it up on my first night home, I found that the connecting hose was of sufficient length to allow me to assume my normal sleeping position on my left side. I wasn't able to do that on the Ward so that was a good start.

I sincerely hope that Dr John will not have to be confronted by the depressing sight of my ugly kisser spoiling the décor of his Ward again. Speaking of which, no praise is too high for the Team who looked after me yet again and got me back on the rails. I was made to feel as though I was the only patient they'd got and nothing was too much trouble. I had the notion that I would like to write about my experiences in the Royal Derby in detail but I didn't think to keep a diary or make notes. Unless you do, it's impossible to remember the names of all the folks who are constantly trooping in and out or the reasons for their visits. They all play their part and all the parts eventually fit together like a jigsaw to form the complete picture, hopefully getting us MFFD and back home again ASAP. Thank you all.

On Wednesday July 15th, my first morning back home, who should turn up at 11:00 but Tom, our District Nurse – a lesson in communication and efficiency if ever there was one. He had called in response to the request from the hospital about the compression stockings because he needed to take my measurements. He checked my blood pressure and oxygen and also the pulses in my legs and was impressed, or so he said. I am allotted two pairs of stockings every six months and the first two pairs were delivered by courier two days later – better than Amazon! That was 3½ years ago and I haven't seen, or heard from, Tom since – I'll take that as a good sign.

Speaking of Tom, my sister Kathleen rang to let us know that my eldest brother Tom had died on Thursday, July 16th, 2020, aged 89, barely 7 months after we'd lost Ken. I hadn't spoken to Tom since Audrey died on August 10th, 2009, so I don't know any of the details surrounding his death except to say that I was given to understand that he had been living in a care home. Once upon a time, I had harboured the idea of boarding a Plymouth-bound train, taking a taxi from the station to Tom's front door and ringing the doorbell. I would have loved to have seen the look on his face when seeing me turn up unannounced, the way he used to do in the old days. In more recent times, however, I have come to accept that such an odyssey is now out of the question – any satisfaction gained would probably be nullified by the stresses of the 500-mile round trip. I struggle to cope even with the thought of the 50-metre round trip to the end of the garden. Even if the trip were still a possibility, it would now be a wasted journey because, sadly, there's nobody home.

Our family connections with Plymouth originally came about as a result of Tom's marriage to Audrey in 1952. They met while Tom was on shore leave in Plymouth whilst serving on the aircraft carrier HMS Indefatigable during his National Service from 1948-50. Audrey's parents and brothers Peter, George and Francis are no longer with us and leave no descendants. Tom's older son Tommy is no longer with us and his descendants are rooted in the USA where he chose to settle down more than 40 years ago. That leaves Tom's younger son David as the sole survivor and he has been resident in Spezet, France for almost 30 years, I believe. I have many memories of all these people over the course of several visits to Plymouth, the first of which was on the occasion of Tom and Audrey's wedding when I was about 6 years old.

There were quite a few of us who had travelled from Borrowash to Plymouth for the occasion. These included Councillor Frank Smith and also best man Albert Anderton, who was married to Tom's cousin, Margaret. I seem to remember that we lodged with a Mrs Cherry and to this day, I don't have the slightest idea who she was or where she lived. Following the wedding, the couple returned to Borrowash to their first marital home at 65, Victoria Avenue, where their first son Tommy was born in 1953. In 1956, they made the move back to Plymouth to a new home at 5, St Michael Avenue, Keyham, where their second son David was born in June, 1960. They lived there until their retirement in 1989, when they decided to move to a bungalow at 112, Bearsdown Road, Eggbuckland. Carole, Richard, Sean and I were their guests there for 2 weeks in 1991, our last visit.

The city of Plymouth has been virtually demolished and rebuilt since the war when so much damage was inflicted by German bombers during the course of their 59 separate attempts to disable the dockyards. In contrast to the concrete and commerce of the city, just a short 15-minute stroll from Royal Parade and we find ourselves on the iconic Plymouth Hoe. This lofty vantage point is dominated by the 25-metre-high Smeaton's Tower, originally designed by John Smeaton as the third of the four lighthouses to be built on the Eddystone Reef, 12 miles offshore in the English Channel. Due to the erosion of the rock on which it was standing, the lighthouse was dismantled in the 1880s and the top two thirds transported to the Hoe stone-by-stone, where it was rebuilt.

Closer inshore, we see Drakes Island and beyond that we see the breakwater, which is some 2 miles from the shore. To our right is the mouth of the River Tamar, gateway to Devonport Dockyard, with the river itself forming the natural border between Devon and Cornwall. Over on the Cornish side of the river we see Mount Edgcumbe Estate, with the tiny village of Cawsand tucked away just out of view and beyond that we see Penlee Point on Rame Head. Over to our left is the rugged Mount Batten peninsular, used as a reconnaissance station and air base by the Royal Navy and the RAF between 1913 and 1986.

Memories of balmy days spent visiting the beautiful Cornish villages of Looe, Cawsand, Polperro, Mevagissey, Fowey – the list is endless. We spent days at Whitsand Bay where Audrey's family owned one of the chalets which were sited along the top of Tregonhawke Cliff, some 350 feet above sea level. There is a winding path which wends its way down the cliff face to the beach where we would plan to spend a full day because negotiating your way down that path and back up again is a once-a-day-only challenge. The 6 miles of south-facing beach was a real sun trap against the cliff face but for the unwary there is a risk, not only of sunburn, but of being cut off by the rising tide.

One of the most vivid memories has to be the day that Tom and I boarded a boat at the Barbican and chugged our way out into the English Channel for a day's fishing. We shared the boat with 3 or 4 other chaps who were all members of the Plymouth Coop Sea Angling Club, of which Tom was the Secretary at that time. Full of anticipation, we set off on the 12-mile trip to the Eddystone Lighthouse in the hope of locating a particular wreck which lies in the shadow of the lighthouse in 35 metres of water. The day turned out to be quite eventful in many ways, not least of which was the weather – hazy sunshine, humid, not a breath of wind and the surface of the water had the appearance of glass. This was deceptive because there was a 10-knot current which took a discarded fag packet away in seconds, plus a 2-metre swell, to boot.

We needed 3 or 4lbs of lead to hold bottom with our mackerel strip bait and this gave the impression that the fish were heavier than they actually were. We trawled the area back and forth but, despite the boat being equipped with sonar, the Skipper couldn't pinpoint the elusive wreck. He probably had one eye on the fuel gauge when we decided to drop anchor to fish the sandy bottom for the day. This yielded mostly bream and whiting and the occasional crab rather than the conger and ling which are known to frequent this wreck, brought to grief on the Eddystone Reef, no doubt.

There were a few becalmed yachts in the area and they were no doubt praying for a breeze to spring up to help them get out of the path of a school of about 12 whales which came too close for comfort. Fortunately, there were no collisions and, for me at least, it was a once-in-a-lifetime opportunity to see these animals in the flesh, breaching and cavorting almost alongside us – spectacular. I hardly ate anything all day because the sultry conditions and the constant rise and fall on the swell spelt queeziness for this landlubber. At the end of the day, the real sea anglers on board were a bit disappointed with the fishing experience but the entertainment provided by the whales was some consolation. I was somewhat relieved to be heading back to port but the fun was not yet over because, as we approached the breakwater, our engine spluttered its last amid a cloud of smoke. Fortunately, we had come back in tandem with another boat and they tossed us a line and towed us back to the Barbican. An unusual day for me and I wouldn't have missed it for the world but I would probably think twice before doing it again, bearing in mind the fact that I can't swim!

CHAPTER 12

During October, 2020, Sean had been experiencing a persistent pain in his left shoulder and he eventually decided to call 111. An ambulance arrived and the crew carried out an ECG before deciding to take him to the hospital for further tests. The diagnosis was pericarditis, or inflammation of the pericardium (the protective membrane which surrounds the heart), the causes of which may be multiple. After spending the afternoon in hospital he was advised to manage it with painkillers and discharged.

On the morning of October 15th, 2020, I had a home visit from Nurse Nikki Dodd from the Royal Derby. She checked my oxygen level, heart rate and blood pressure and also took a blood sample from my ear lobe. This was analysed on the spot while we waited and the readings were fine. She also issued me with a "salbutamol" inhaler, to be used should I experience congestion and/or breathing problems. I think the main reason for this visit was to gather up-to-date info in preparation for my telephone appointment with Dr James Donaldson, which was scheduled for 11:00 on November 6th. He is a member of the respiratory Team on Ward 403 but I couldn't recall having met him before. His call was punctual and we spoke for 5 minutes about my progress over the 4 months since my discharge. From my point of view, I was satisfied and relieved with the way things had gone, both with the mask and the oximeter readings and had not encountered any problems that I was aware of. He was satisfied with things from his point of view, in particular the hours that I was registering on the NIV machine – this info is relayed direct to the hospital from the NIV. The blood test result was satisfactory and he suggested a further appointment in 6 months, i.e. May, 2021.

By January, 2021, the covid vaccination program was gathering momentum and Carole was invited to attend the Derby Arena on January 28th (1st jab) and again on April 15th (2nd jab). Transport was provided courtesy of a local taxi service, for which there was no direct charge to the patient. This excellent service was recommended to us by the surgery and Carole was the only passenger in the same 12-seater minibus with the same driver on both occasions. I thought I had made it clear that I was quite prepared to travel to my local surgery but not as far afield as Derby or any other far-flung province. Somebody kindly took it upon themselves to label me "housebound", as a result of which, two different nurses came all the way from Chesterfield to give me my jabs, the first one on February 7th and the second on April 26th. We managed to make appointments at Borrowash for our boosters on October 21st for Carole, and on December 4th for me.

The spring of 2021 saw the arrival on the patio of a female blackbird with most unusual plumage. I imagined that she may have been one of last years' chicks on the lookout for a mate and suitable territory. Her colouring was quite normal except that each of her wings had a row of four, equi-spaced white lines running across it between the shoulder and the tip. These marks were about ½" long and to my eyes, they formed a perfectly symmetrical pattern when she was at rest. A white feather or two in a blackbird's plumage is quite common but eight marks forming such a perfect pattern seems astonishing, if not unique. For fairly obvious reasons, we immediately decided to name her "Missy Whitestripes". At first, she appeared nervous and unsure of herself and if the resident female blackbird appeared, Missy would make herself scarce until the coast was clear.

As the days went by she seemed to grow in confidence and became much more assertive and she herself was now discouraging intruders. I was convinced that she was looking to take over as our lady of the manor, though at this stage she didn't appear to have a mate. Unfortunately, things didn't quite work out for her because one day she appeared in a somewhat dishevelled and disorientated state and she had a bulge on her breast, which I was hoping may just be displaced feathers. It was apparent that there had been an incident of some sort which seemed to change the whole complexion of things. She didn't appear to be injured but it seemed to me that she may have been involved in a squabble, or cat attack, or maybe she had collided with something, though that isn't very likely. Her confidence had obviously taken a blow and she was now an unsettled bird who readily took flight if disturbed, usually heading over the fence into Kevin's bramble patch. Whenever she appeared on the patio, she was usually ushered away by the resident female until one day in April, 2021, she disappeared and didn't return.

We'd been putting out food and water for the hedgehogs for a couple of years and become accustomed to seeing them turn up for an evening snack. We knew that there were at least three hogs because sometimes they would all arrive together and the biggest of them was a bit of a bully. We named him "Bumbly Bully" as he wasn't too keen on sharing the food and didn't hesitate in head-butting and bulldozing the slightly smaller hogs away from the food (pellets and dried mealworms). They would simply curl up and wait patiently until he'd had his fill and gone on his way and they didn't appear to come to any real harm.

Of the two smaller hogs, the most frequent visitor we named "Tiggy". On reflection, we thought this one might also be a male because Bumbly would quickly bully him into submission but that was usually the end of the matter. Tiggy had not been absent for a long-enough period of time to have given birth to a litter and we'd not seen any hoglets either. A fourth hog joined the trio at one stage and this one was now the smallest – it had a cute, fluffy face and if ever any hog could be called pretty, this was the one. We stretched our imagination to its limits and named it "Fluffyface" and, for two or three weeks, it turned up at about 21:00 as regularly as clockwork. We had got used to looking out for it scurrying down the path at dusk until one evening, it failed to appear. We never saw it again and have no way of knowing what became of it – maybe it had a mishap or simply moved on to pastures new?

We first became aware of "Ginger" the fox during the first few days of May, 2021. For a while we'd suspected that there might be fox activity in the garden and our suspicions were proved right when Carole came upon what looked like a den tucked away in the corner of the garden, behind the holly bush. It was sheltered under the hawthorn hedge and the fences and the undergrowth had been flattened. There were a couple of kiddies' toys close by, the theft of which is a common trait among foxes, or so we read, and it all looked very cosy. When Ginger first ventured to the patio she was wary and conscious of the light from the lounge window and if she detected the slightest movement, she was gone in a flash. Her skittish behaviour made us wonder if there might be a cub waiting somewhere in the darkness?

Just after 21:00 on the evening of May 21st, after I'd gone up to bed, Carole saw a fox on the patio which she said was much smaller than Ginger and she thought that it could be a cub but it seemed to be on its own. A week went by before I got my first sighting of our new visitor and it definitely seemed to be a cub, about the same size as the cats that come prowling. We suspected that Ginger would be close by somewhere in the shadows and on the occasions when she did appear, she would sniff the cub in a sort of reassuring greeting. She would hover briefly before ambling to the sidelines where she would wait patiently until the cub had finished eating and the pair would then disappear into the night. There was an obvious bond between them and we were fortunate enough to witness it at such close quarters. It was only when I saw them together that I realised that neither appeared to have the iconic white tip to their tail and it seemed apt to name the cub "Notip".

As the evenings went by, Ginger became a little more relaxed but never really overcame her wariness and she seemed reluctant to raise her gaze to make full eye contact – it was more of an "over-her-specs" look. Occasionally, for no apparent reason, she would lose her nerve and disappear, as if she sensed that something wasn't quite right. Notip was growing, both in size and confidence, and there was very little hesitation or fear in her cheeky gaze – she favoured full face, eye-to-eye contact. I suppose the difference between them was that Notip had been used to the site of us at close quarters from about 2 months old but it was almost certainly a new experience for Ginger.

There were a couple of clues which led me to believe that Notip may well have been female. Even with my untrained eye I could see that she had grown by Christmas, by which time she would be about 8 months old, but then didn't seem to grow any more. She was now a striking, well-proportioned individual with a beautiful-looking, tan coat and tail and there seemed to be a paler, golf-ball-sized patch of fur on her right hip. She was still not as big as Ginger and this suggested two things to me: 1) Notip was possibly now fully-grown and female and 2) Ginger may actually be the father rather than the mother? We also noticed that Notip crouched when weeing, as ladies usually do, though we read that this is not a foolproof clue when trying to assess the gender of a fox.

It was now New Year, 2022 and the foxes were into their breeding season. We were hearing the yapping of the dog foxes and occasional blood-curdling screams from the vixens at all hours of the night. I believe this is the vixens' response to the dogs who are on the lookout for a mate. It may have been my imagination but I seemed to sense a change in attitude from our foxes during that period. We had become accustomed to Notip's eye-to-eye contact, pausing briefly as she ate to check us out. She didn't seem as sociable now, with barely a glance as she grabbed a quick snack before trotting off into the night. Her visits had become less frequent and she always seemed to be in a hurry, as if she had more important business elsewhere.

We'd seen her on most evenings since May, 2021, watching her blossom and grow and she had almost become part of the family but we haven't had a positive sighting of her since April 8th, 2022. We don't know if there is a connection but this is about the time that fox cubs are usually born but we hadn't seen any evidence that she had a mate. Perhaps she simply wasn't ready for breeding yet? If all the available dogs find a mate then there obviously won't be enough to go around, leaving the lone females assigned to nursemaiding duties, at least for this, her first year?

The day before Notip's disappearance, a new fox had appeared in the garden during the evening of April 7th, 2022. This one was about the same size as Notip but scrawnier-looking and underweight, with tufts in its skinny tail, which was also devoid of any white tip. It looked a bit of a waif who was in need of a good square meal and grooming but it had a nice, friendly face. Its wispy-looking coat had dark roots and was more ginger than tan in colour. It appeared most evenings, usually before dusk and often with Ginger, suggesting that it may be Notip's sibling and we suspected that it spent the days snoozing in Kevin's tumbledown shed. It wasn't long before it found its way to the patio to sample the pellets and dried mealworms and was soon a regular visitor who didn't seem at all bothered that it had an audience. We thought our new visitor should be named "Dainty", mainly because it was slight in stature but this one also crouches to wee and may be female as well?

On the morning of Saturday, April 22nd, 2022, we had a pleasant surprise when our estranged blackbird, Missy Whitestripes, turned up on the patio. She had been driven out 11 months ago and went into exile but now she was back, this time accompanied by a sleek-looking mate. We named him "Mr Whitestripes" and they were a handsome pair if ever there was one and he followed her everywhere. It was good to see her looking fit and well again and it seemed that she hadn't forgotten our patch. She appeared to have made a full recovery from last years' mystery experience and the two of them looked as though they were here on unfinished business. Their task was made easier when the resident pair decided to relocate to a neighbouring garden to start their breeding campaign. I suspect that they may have been wary of the squirrels that had moved into the conifers beneath the sycamore, where we know blackbirds have nested in the past. Missy came to the patio on most days and everything seemed to be going well – I actually spotted her taking nesting material into those same conifers. Maybe she wasn't too concerned about the squirrels, who are known to be quite partial to half a dozen new-laid eggs.

On the afternoon of Saturday, May 21st, 2022, however, the situation suddenly changed. I saw Missy arrive on the patio for a snack and when she'd done, she headed for the gap between the forsythia and the orange blossom. A visiting cat must have spotted her feeding and, unbeknown to us, had hidden itself behind the low wall at the edge of the patio only 2 or 3 metres away. As Missy took off, the cat's random flail somehow found the target and she was downed. I flung the door open and, mercifully, that seemed to be enough to distract and panic the cat into taking flight, leaving Missy lying on her side on the concrete amidst 3 or 4 flight feathers and some down. She was obviously shocked but as I made my way towards her, she managed to take off to seek refuge in the sycamore. She appeared to be OK but it all happened so quickly that I couldn't be sure that she wasn't injured. Alas, that was the last time we saw her and her bid for our patch had been thwarted yet again and we could only hope and pray that she would recover. Mr Whitestripes continues to share the garden quite happily with the resident pair and is still on his own. Maybe he is hoping that Missy will come home – she's done it before.

For some weeks, Carole had been experiencing aches and pains around the top of her legs and hips and was struggling to walk any distance.

Eventually, she decided to call the surgery and was given a phone appointment with Dr Joshi for May 25th, 2022. Following a brief discussion, Dr Joshi said that she would refer Carole to the hospital but, in the meantime, she should make an appointment at the surgery for a physical examination. She saw Dr Day on May 26th for this examination and she thought that Carole should go to the Long Eaton Health Centre for a pelvic X-ray and she would put in the request. Carole rang the LEHC and she was given an appointment for Wednesday, June 1st, 2022, at 12:00. The X-ray revealed fractures in three adjoining vertebrae but there was no way of telling how or when this damage had occurred. She was advised to lead her life as normal and has had no further treatment.

At 10:30 on the morning of Saturday, July 2nd, 2022, an injured fox turned up on the patio. Didn't recognise this one – it looked older and was underweight and carrying its right foreleg, bent at the wrist joint. It was able to straighten the joint but was reluctant to put any weight on the leg and it seemed to be drinking a lot but showed no interest in the pellets. It had doleful eyes and skinny hind legs and it looked to be in a poor state of health generally and it spent the day resting in the garden, making frequent visits to the water bowls. By afternoon it was looking a bit brighter and grooming itself and had managed to eat a few worms and pellets. These were positive signs, so fingers crossed. As I watched it drink, it appeared to me that the water level in the bowl was not going down and that made me think it might be lapping but not actually swallowing? It was also pausing now and again, allowing water to drip from its mouth as if it might be helping to sooth a toothache? This may have been preventing it from eating properly and could explain why the animal was underweight – then again, this is pure conjecture and probably bunkum.

The fox disappeared overnight and we didn't see it on the Sunday – maybe it had moved on? Not likely – it turned up again at 09:00 on Monday morning (the 4th) and spent another day in the garden, drinking but not eating much. It was still carrying the leg but getting about OK, managing to break into a three-legged lope when it heard Carole go out to the dustbin. It was grooming and appeared to be perfectly alert – maybe it was the paw that was the problem rather than the leg? It ate a few pellets at teatime before settling down for a couple of hours in the evening sunshine, eventually leaving at 19:30, and heading off towards the road. That was the last we saw of it and we can only hope that we may have done our bit to help it on its way to recovery.

On a happier note, it was now 3 months since Dainty first appeared and we'd got used to seeing her on most evenings, sometimes with Ginger but more recently on her own. She amused herself by having the odd unsuccessful shy at the birds or the squirrels, or even the blackbird-killer cat that spends its days in our garden. She seemed to enjoy playing with a couple of balls which had appeared in the garden over recent weeks and we also found kiddies' dolls here and there which had undoubtedly been left by the foxes. We last saw Ginger on April 28th and, subsequently, Dainty seemed to have the garden to herself, until the morning of Monday, July 11th. Carole was up early (about 05:00) and saw two foxes play-fighting and rolling around on the lawn. She thought one of them was Dainty but didn't recognise the other one but the white fur on its throat caught her eye. The pair were seen in the early mornings for about a week but then we didn't see either of them for about three weeks, when I caught a glimpse of a fox as it trotted across the patio and then off down the garden. I suspect it was Dainty's new friend but couldn't be sure.

CHAPTER 13

As I write this on Wednesday, July 13th, 2022, it is one year to the day since Carole and I visited the Anderson Electrical Arena in Spondon to meet Alan Ure, Secretary and General Manager of Borrowash Victoria AFC. This meeting came about as a result of my fumbling about on t'internet looking at pictures of Borrowash village. I stumbled upon a captioned image which showed some Vics' members taking a refreshments break whilst on a Club outing to Skeggy. What caught my eye was the caption above it which listed the names of the players and Committee members which were featured on an adjoining photo. My name was amongst them but unfortunately the actual image had been guillotined. We contacted the Vics about it and Alan invited us to visit the ground to view the missing image in the Club History Book, hence the aforementioned meeting, arranged for Wednesday, July 14th, 2021, at 09:30. He was actually on pitch-mowing duty at the time and, after showing us to our reserved table in the deserted Clubroom, he mounted his mower and left us to browse the History Book at our leisure.

We soon found the "photo", which was dated 1967/68 but I suspect it may have been the season before? It wasn't of the best quality, akin to a negative or pencil sketch and a copy of it was not really an option. After spending a few minutes browsing we were about to leave when the legendary Ian Anderson appeared, accompanied by his grandson. I knew Ian by sight and reputation because of his long association with the Club but had never had the pleasure of meeting him. His arrival seemed too well timed to have been coincidence and I think he must have been tipped off about our visit. He mentioned that the History Book needed updating and that he and former Secretary Ian Collins had intended to do it. Their plans failed to materialise, however, because after a 30-year association with the Club, Mr Collins chose to move on in 2014. Ian Anderson was easy to talk to and made us feel welcome but he couldn't offer us tea and biscuits because there was no milk! He did, however, promise to pass on our good wishes to everyone, particularly Derek Dickenson, who he sees most weeks either on the golf course, in the pub, or on the touchline.

Despite the disappointment of the photo we were glad we made the trip but the search for the original was now on in earnest because I simply had to have a copy. I wrote a letter of thanks to Alan, enclosing a small donation as a gesture of appreciation for his hospitality and our continued support of Borrowash Vics. It was somewhat disappointing to learn that my letter had been delivered in error to a neighbouring address but, thanks to the kind lady of the house, it was eventually delivered safely but only after she had opened it with her big nose. I received a note of thanks from Ian, who I believe is currently Vice Chairman of the Club, and he assured me that he would send me a fixture list, which I never received. I did, however, receive a letter from Derek on August 19th, 2021, which was commendably and impressively hand-written, and I replied to it the following week. I received a second letter from Derek on September 23rd, and I replied to that the following week. Both these lines of communication have since gone very quiet and I've heard nothing more from Ian and very little from Derek.

I also messaged Doug Smith on September 24th, the first contact since our rendezvous in Borrowash in July, 2019, and we thought that perhaps we ought to meet up again in the New Year. I received a Xmas card from him on December 21st but have heard nothing since. With Sean's help, the miracle of electronic gadgetry and a slice of luck we managed to trace the photo, which had originally been posted on FB by the late John Dilley, apparently. From that we managed to produce an excellent copy of the original, which is now framed and proudly displayed on my lounge wall. It was definitely taken at Deans Drive, though I have no recollection of the occasion and was not even aware of its existence until I came upon it purely by accident. I'll always be grateful to John's daughter Melanie, without whose help none of this would have been possible and I wouldn't have this precious memento, which is now proudly displayed on my lounge wall.

Our grandson Jim took his GCSEs in June, 2022, the results of which were published on Thursday, August 25th, 2022. His close friend Silvie Kurcevicz achieved the top set of grades at their Brookfield School with five 9s and three 8s, just pipping Jim into second place with his four 9s and four 8s. He continues to make excellent progress academically and we are all impressed by his mature and positive attitude. He has gained the respect of both his peers and his seniors and that speaks volumes for his character and background. Where all this will lead is anybody's guess but he is laying down good solid foundations and is well organised.

Richard took to writing as a hobby in the late 1990s and from time to time has attempted to arouse the interest of various publishers. It was only recently that he became aware of a self-publishing scheme which is run in conjunction with Amazon. He decided to give it a try and since August, 2021, he has had eight novels published, with sales now totalling over 100. I believe the book-price is based on Amazon's production costs plus VAT and a nominal royalty for the author. Feedback from his readers has been positive and has given him renewed enthusiasm and belief after so much disappointment in the past. His published titles thus far are Deliver Us from Evil, Within These Walls, Hells Gate, Swans at Clearlake, Last of the Old School, In Plain Sight, A Prayer for Martin and No More Tea and Toast. He has also written biographical studies of Les Dawson, Brian Clough and Freddie Mercury but publishers insist that personal material of this sort must have family consent before they make any commitment. That sounds reasonable but is easier said than done because contacting the people concerned can prove to be difficult. I'm sure that Richard has more in the pipeline and, fingers crossed, he will come up with the big one before long.

Following our visit to the Vics on July 14th, 2021, I messaged Alan Ure on September 24th to ask if there was any possibility that I might acquire a personal copy of the Vics' History Book. I fully expected, for one reason or another, that his response would be negative but I couldn't have been more wrong. Phrases like "leave it with me – no problem" and "I'll sort it". Progress was only steady because, in addition to his Club duties, he was toing and froing to his parents' home in Scotland most weeks and he must have been pushed for spare time.

At about 07:30 on Tuesday, September 20th, 2022, we noticed a fox, which we didn't recognise, lying stretched out on its belly at the bottom of the garden. It appeared to be snoozing but then, very gingerly, it got to its feet and started to make its way onto the lawn. It was moving in very unsteady fairy steps and it was obvious that this was a sick animal and it only managed to stagger 3 or 4 metres before going down on its belly again. We could see that its breathing was laboured but it managed to get to its feet a second time to make a further 2 metres to the path, near the bird baths. It stood motionless for a minute or two before going down on its belly again and within a short time it had stopped breathing. This was a distressing incident which we won't ever forget but when we called the Council regarding disposal, the advice was to "just double-bag it and put it in the black bin". Thanks.

During the afternoon of Wednesday, October 19th, another fox appeared in the garden in broad daylight. It had lost most of its fur save for some around its neck and breast and the white tip of its tail. It was underweight and struggling to walk and looked to my untrained eye like a classic case of mange. It was sad to see it looking so naked and submissive – you can see it in their eyes. It made its way slowly to the patio to eat some mealworms and its skin looked dry and sore. It appeared again three days later and was making its way towards the patio until I quietly opened the door to put out some more pellets. Despite my stealth, it must have heard me because it turned tail and disappeared and I didn't see it again until 21:00 on October 27th. After watching it for a while as it tucked into the mealworms, I went up to bed with the thought that it would struggle when the weather turned colder. We saw it on November 3rd and 7th (when we named it "Tiny Tim") and again for the last time on January 5th, 2023, when he came for breakfast.

By October the bats and hedgehogs had retired for the winter and the blackbirds and starlings only came occasionally, though Mr Whitestripes turned up most days, still on his own. That situation changed on August 30th, however, when the resident Mr Blackbird was ambushed and stolen by the same cat that had attacked Missy Whitestripes. We think that the resident female blackbird and Mr Whitestripes, having both lost their mates to that same cat, decided to team up and went on to produce their first brood in the spring of 2023. A starling with an injured foot was a regular visitor to the patio but we've not noticed it for about 5 weeks now. Hopefully it's healed and the bird is indistinguishable from the rest of the gang? The irrepressible squirrels are back to normal – they are inseparable and spend their days racing, chasing and wrestling. Their display of speed and agility is certainly a sight to behold.

On Wednesday, October 13th, 2022, Sean went to the hospital after feeling unwell since the previous weekend. He was detained overnight for observation and the following day (Thursday) was transferred to Sheffield for more tests, before being discharged on the Friday. It appeared that he had experienced a bleed between his skull and his brain (rather than IN his brain) but it had now stopped leaking and healed itself, apparently. Tests, thorough though they seemed to be, nevertheless proved inconclusive and the cause remains unexplained. The medical advice was that he should go about his business as usual as it is unlikely that this will happen again and, thankfully, he has had no further problem.

Sarah was due to start a new job on Monday, October 18th, but with Sean being in dock, that was postponed until the following Monday. She is now in the employ of Derbyshire County Council working as an advisor on matters of health and wellbeing. This entails offering support and advice to folks who are trying to give up smoking, lose weight, etc. and generally making an effort to improve their quality of life. She took part in the Derby Half Marathon on November 29th, and achieved a personal milestone by completing the course, from Derby city centre to Elvaston Castle and back, non-stop. Sean had been due to accompany her on the run but wasn't yet fit enough, though he was on hand in the roll of her supporter-in-chief on what was a pretty cold day.

On Saturday, October 16th, 2021, I was up at around 01:00 for my tea and cereals and, on pulling back the curtain, I saw Tiggy by the water bowl. When I went out to him with more worms he was making a whimpering noise and it was only then that I realised that he was injured and in some distress. His nearside hind leg was sticking straight out behind him and he appeared to be trying to get into the water, perhaps in an effort to sooth the leg? It appeared to me that the leg must be dislocated or broken and he was obviously having difficulty getting about. I imagined that the chances of recovery from such an injury must be rather slim in the wild. I watched as he shuffled away into the night at around 02:30, and the overriding thought was the possibility that we may not see him again. Are we supposed to contact the Rescue Centre? I doubt that they would respond if the animal was mobile because he could be anywhere by the time they turned up and it would be like looking for a hedgehog in a haystack. The prospect of not seeing Tiggy again was extremely sad – it is all too easy to become attached to these animals. It's OK until something goes wrong, as it too often does in their world, and it's sometimes difficult to know what to do for the best. At the end of the day they are wild and, unless they are in immediate physical danger, I think it's probably better in the long run to let nature take its course.

Five days later, on Thursday, October 21st, against all hopes and expectations, who should arrive for supper at 20:00 but Tiggy! By some miracle, the injured leg seemed to be back in its proper place and, though it must have been pretty difficult, he had summoned up the will and determination to get to the food and water supply. I have no idea where his daytime retreat is but he had shown remarkable courage for one so comparatively small. We saw him again on the Friday and Saturday and those were the last sightings until March 9th, 2022. He had survived the winter hibernation period and made a full recovery from what had appeared to be a horrific injury.

We had grown accustomed to the sight of squirrels scampering around the neighbourhood in their never-ending search for food, territory and mischief and they were frequent visitors to our birdfeeders. We usually had plenty of food available so we didn't mind them adding a few titbits to their diet but it's a bit annoying when they chew the plastic around the feeder ports. They attack the bits that hold it all together until it collapses and the wreckage then has to be replaced, which is costly. During the autumn/winter months of 2021/22, two of them decided that our patch was squirrels' paradise and they took up residence. They built their drey in the upper branches of Kevin's towering sycamore tree (Kevin is our next door neighbour) and it must have been 40 feet above the ground.

They spent their days foraging, wrestling and charging around the garden nose-to-tail at breakneck speed – they were inseparable. I've watched them sprinting through the branches of what's left of our rotting hawthorn hedge and their agility is truly remarkable. The spring of 2022 arrived with a spell of windy weather and the drey was taking quite a buffeting and beginning to disintegrate. They were forced to relocate and were seen taking building stuff into the conifers which surround the base of the sycamore trunk – they are 4 metres tall and virtually weatherproof. It wasn't long before we were seeing only one squirrel and we wondered if there may be some kittens on the way? We were now into July and hadn't noticed any sign of an increase in numbers and still saw only one squirrel at any one time. We don't know if it was the same one or if they took it in turns to appear?

Yet another dental appointment on Friday, October 15th, 2021, this time with Dr Rafia Hamid. My last appointment with Dr Poonam Chudasama was in March and she had told me that she would be leaving in June to join a Practice in Birmingham. She was also due to be married there later in the year. Despite having been a regular patient at Moores Practice for almost 60 years, it's a still a ball-ache whenever my appointment is due. Dr Hamid seemed to have a down-to-earth, practical approach and she suggested putting a temporary filling in my broken tooth rather than trying to extract what's left of it. Thursday, October 21st, 2021 was an important date, not only for little Tiggy Hedgehog, but also because we made the trip to Borrowash surgery for Carole's covid booster jab appointment. This was a 60-minute round trip of 13 miles, including 30 minutes waiting time, just for the sake of a little prick – say no more. Back to the dentist's for my temporary filling on December 3rd – my next appointment is scheduled for March 4th, 2022. Following my trip to the dentist on the 3rd, we were back at Borrowash surgery at 09:55 the following morning, Saturday the 4th, for my covid booster.

At midday on Monday, February 28th, 2022, I received a phone call from the Moores Dental Practice informing me that my appointment on March 4th, less than four days hence, would have to be cancelled. Dr Hamid had apparently "moved on", rather suddenly it seems, and there was no one available to replace her, at least for the foreseeable future. I was told that I would remain registered as an NHS patient and, if the situation changed, I would be contacted with regard to a new appointment. After due consideration, I decided to air my views regarding the unacceptable situation which was developing, not only in NHS dentistry but also in General Practice. On March 10th, I wrote to the Practice Manager at Moores, to Maggie Throup MP and also to Sajid Javid, the Health Secretary.

Two months later, on Saturday, May 14th, I received a belated reply from Sarah Smith, the Practice Manager, which told me nothing that I hadn't already managed to work out for myself. It did, however, confirm that I would remain registered with the Practice as an NHS patient. In the meantime, should I require emergency treatment, I would be able to make an appointment with one of the remaining Practice at a convenient time. Just what that means remains to be seen. Two of the seven dentists at Moores Practice have left in the past two years, one having "moved on" and the other having retired, and neither has been replaced. As a result of this situation, 5,000 appointments per year have been forfeited at this Practice alone, affecting 1,500 patients.

As of today's date, July 23rd, 2022, I have not received any response from my MP or the Health Secretary, which is no surprise – two more stamps wasted. Tens of thousands of NHS patients just like me are being dumped, deprived of access to treatment and left with little choice other than to resort to "private practice", or suffer. Many of us simply cannot afford the cost of private health care and, until such time as the NHS is finally knocked on the head, we are being denied our rights. NHS patients are being held to ransom by Government and Practitioners whose joint devotion to financial gain obviously takes precedence over any obligation to either the NHS or its patients. Surely, this was precisely the reason that the NHS was founded in the first place, in order that anyone and everyone, regardless of status or financial situation, would have access to "free at source" medical and dental care?

Whilst the NHS remains operational, the intolerable situation which has been allowed, even blatantly encouraged, to develop is not only immoral but unethical. It is highly likely that it is also illegal, in that we continue to pay the same taxes despite the fact that these vital services are being systematically withdrawn and therefore require less funding. A possible solution to the dilemma lies in the hands of the patients themselves. It is within their power to put an end to this divisive two-tier system by boycotting private practice, with immediate effect, and ultimately making it unlawful. Any Practitioners who then do not wish to work exclusively for the NHS will, of course, be free to pursue alternative careers. Speaking of which, Sarah decided on a career change and, as of January 16th, 2023, she has been employed by a charity organisation known as "Action for Children". Its aim is to help deal with the problems faced by needy and underprivileged children.

On Monday, March 28th, 2022, I received a message from Alan Ure to say that he had completed my copy of the History Book and that he would deliver it, if I so wished. On the following Monday, April 4th, Carole and I were about to sit down for lunch at 11:30 when a large, white vehicle drew up at the kerbside. The driver emerged and as he turned and made his way towards our door, I recognised him as Alan, my new-found friend at Borrowash Vics. As I greeted him, I could see my copy of the Vics' History Book clenched in his large, Scottish fist. Six months had gone by and I couldn't believe that he'd managed to complete the task, thus making me one of a select band of people to possess a personal copy. I was so pleased that he'd taken the time and trouble to call but he didn't linger as he was just about to set off on the 6-hour journey to Scotland to visit his parents. Before I knew it, he was on his way northward in his large, white, purring Jaguar. I wrote to him on April 8th, this time at his home address, to thank him for his time and effort in producing and delivering my Book. Once again, I enclosed a small donation as a gesture of thanks and continued support of Borrowash Vics.

After reading through the History Book, there were a couple of things which stood out to me, the most obvious being that it hadn't been updated since the 1985/86 season. The present-day records begin with season 1963/64, the first season that we played under the revived name of Borrowash Victoria AFC. Once upon a time, there was a gang of teenagers who frequented Borrowash Youth Club on Friday evenings. It was suggested that we had enough interested players amongst our membership to start our own football team and thus, in 1960, Borrowash Youth Club FC was born.

We spent our first season playing friendly matches against some of the established local teams such as Ockbrook, Draycott, Long Eaton Magpies and Spondon Dynamos, to name but a few. We were pleased with our results and decided to apply to join the Derby Welfare League for the season 1961/62. Our application was duly accepted and we started our League life in Section F, the bottom division where all new teams started. I remember the feeling of anticipation and exhilaration as our first match approached – even better than sex, some silly bugger said. Our first game was played on the old pitch at Deans Drive in September, 1961, against fellow newcomers Brunswick Rangers FC, from Derby. The result was a 5–5 draw in a humdinger of a game, enjoyed by both sets of players and the few spectators alike.

Derby Welfare League results were usually published in the Derby Evening Telegraph on the Monday following Saturday's games. Over our first two League seasons the results were encouraging and they had obviously been noticed because we received an approach from Mr Albert Anderton with regard to forming a Committee to look after team affairs. Albert was well-known in the village and had a long association with previous Vics' teams and was a member of the Club when they won the Derby Welfare League Championship in 1952. He was obviously a voice of experience and so his offer was accepted and he promptly recruited Oswald Whyman and Neville Hardy as cohorts and the three of them formed our Management Committee.

Almost immediately, the Committee put forward the suggestion that perhaps we should adopt the original name of "Borrowash Victoria AFC", the traditional name by which the village football teams had always been known. That was approved and the League were notified regarding the change of name in time for the start of the new season, 1963/64. There is a well-publicised, misleading story that Borrowash Vics had "replaced" Borrowash Youth Club in the League but, in fact, this is a myth. The squad of players going into the 1963/64 season was basically the same as it had been for the previous three seasons – we had simply changed the Club name. It is somewhat disappointing that only scant reference is made to those first three seasons when we played as Borrowash Youth Club FC, in view of the significant part they played in the rebirth of the Club as we know it today.

During our visit to the Vics' ground in July, 2021, Ian Anderson had mentioned the fact that the History Book needed updating but I didn't realise at the time what an understatement that was. The records begin with the 1963/64 season, which was the first season that we played under the revived name of Borrowash Victoria AFC. At the moment, it covers the period from then until the end of the 1985/86 season, thanks mainly to the efforts of former Club Chairman Keith Tyler. Since he left the Committee in 1986, updating of the Book has, sadly and unforgivably, been neglected. In June, 2022, I offered to at least make a start on continuing Keith's good work, subject to the Club records still being accessible, but I didn't get any response.

CHAPTER 14

I had a pleasant surprise on the evening of Tuesday, May 17th, 2022 when, out of the blue, I received a text message from Mike Ronan, our first contact since December, 2018. He said he hadn't forgotten about me but what with the covid business and also his hip and heart issues, things had got derailed and the time had just flown by. He knew that I wasn't well the last time we spoke and hoped that I was coping and perhaps I'd get in touch again soon. I replied promptly and he called me at 11:00 the following day to tell me that he is in the process of completing his autobiography and had just returned from a meeting with the printers. We chatted for 20 minutes, mainly about old times, and he mentioned that John Ashman had died in 2016. Mike had been due to have hip surgery but that had been delayed for various reasons. He asked if I would like a copy of his book when it is published and he would be in touch again about that. For the time being though, things seemed to be a bit up in the air so we left it at that and will hopefully speak again soon. That was 18 months ago and I haven't heard anything more but hopefully things are getting sorted. I didn't feel inclined to contact him because it sounded as though he'd got enough on his plate and I put my trust in the old adage that "no news is good news".

My follow-up telephone appointment with Dr Donaldson, originally scheduled for May, 2021, had been delayed due to the covid backlog but we finally made contact when he called at 10:40 on April 22nd, 2022. He was happy with the feedback from the NIV unit and seemed satisfied with my progress. He did mention, however, that I hadn't had a capillary (ear lobe) blood test since Nurse Nikki visited me on October 15th, 2020. He was quick to point out that, due to too much staff flow and not enough cash flow, a home visit would not be possible at this time and I would need to go to the hospital for the test. I explained that I was a reluctant traveller these days and such a trip may prove stressful and his response was that we'd just have to manage without the test and that was that. I'm not sure about the significance of this test or what it actually tells us but apparently we can manage without it? He suggested that we speak again in a year's time, unless there was a problem in the meantime.

On Monday, June 13th, 2022, my sister Kathleen called with the dreadful news that Harry had suffered a heart attack that morning and didn't recover. The two of them were getting ready to go out for a walk and Harry was in the bedroom when Kath heard a noise. When she went to investigate, she found Harry lying on his back on the bed, apparently asleep. She said it looked as though he had been sitting on the edge of the bed and just laid back and nodded off but there was no response when she spoke to him and she quickly realised why. Not a good start to the day and in that situation, I should imagine it must be difficult to think clearly and be able to decide what to do first. Perhaps it's a blessing that she has family close by for support, should she need it. The Harry that I knew was probably one of the most even-tempered men I ever met and never seemed to have a bad word to say about anybody. Such qualities are all too rare these days and in that respect, Harry and Dennis (Porter), my other brother-in-law, must be tied for the gold medal. The funeral service was held on June 28th – safe journey, Harry. Up the Argyle! (and The Rams).

On Tuesday, June 28th, 2022, Carole and I took a taxi ride to Breaston Pharmacy for our covid boosters. Thursday, July 14th, 2022, was quite a significant date because this was the last date on which the printed version of the Long Eaton Website Extra was distributed. This newspaper, founded in 2009, was a welcome innovation following the demise of the Long Eaton Advertiser in October, 2008. It is really disappointing that the LE Website Extra is no longer available in the shops, though it is still available on t'internet. The problems which local businesses encountered during the covid pandemic resulted in a drop in the advertising revenue which provided vital funding for the newspaper. On Wednesday, July 27th, 2022, our neighbour Dave at No 16 came home from work at lunchtime and, after taking some boxes from the boot of his car to the garage, he disappeared and we haven't seen anything of him since? The following day, a young lady wearing a dog-tag ID badge arrived and spent half-an-hour searching through his car. We got the impression that she may have been a police officer?

On October 20th, 2022, our newly-selected Prime Minister Liz Truss eventually bowed to common sense and decency when she announced her resignation. This was inevitable following six weeks of utter chaos following her official appointment by the Queen on September 6th, 2022. Predictably, it hadn't take long for her Prime Ministerial wheels to come off but she did, however, manage to win acclaim for her cameo performance as Maggie Thatcher. Not in the same league as Boris's Churchillian overtures but at least it's something to tell the grandkids about – maybe she has a future on the stage? After dismissing the half-hearted, stalking-horse leadership contenders Penny Mordaunt and Boris Johnson, Rishi Sunak was selected unopposed. He was officially appointed PM by King Charles on October 25th, 2022.

Over a period of weeks, Carole and I had been thinking about getting rid of the car and in July, 2022, we decided that we would be able to manage without it. Following my hospitalisation in January, 2019, our typical motoring mileage had dwindled to about 6 miles per week. As I no longer made the daily, 2-mile return trips to the newsagents it was the weekly trip to Tesco for the main shopping, usually early on a Wednesday morning, which accounted for that. There was the odd outing to Breaston or Borrowash for medical appointments but they were few and far between. Over the recent two-year period we had been plagued by problems of a flat battery nature and were forced to call the Garage for assistance on three occasions. The first time it happened it was a nuisance but the second time, and then a third time, it had become an annoyance and an embarrassment.

On the first occasion we were in Tesco car park and just about to return home from the weekly shopping trip. Long Eaton Garage Services responded promptly to our mayday call to give us a jump start so that we were able to follow them back to base. After testing the battery we opted to replace it at a cost of about £100 but the new battery soon began to deteriorate in similar fashion. We had to call the Garage on two more occasions just as we were about to leave home for appointments. From then on, I'm afraid that I'd come to expect that the battery would be flat whenever the car was needed and I no longer trusted it. The problem arose initially because we were not doing sufficient mileage in order to maintain the charge in the battery. We made an effort to try and solve that by taking Sunday morning drives to Draycott. Neither Carole nor I had either the inclination or the enthusiasm for such a chore and I'm sure that we both had better ways to spend our time. I derived no pleasure at all from being on the roads in today's conditions and the battery problems only added to my hesitance. I still consider myself to be a safe, competent and courteous driver but that can't be said of some of those that we have to share the roads with today.

We had discussed the weekly shopping trip and decided that it could be solved by availing ourselves of the excellent online ordering and delivery service that we know Tesco provide. We make regular use of the taxi service in the town and find it reliable, obliging and seemingly always available. We have the local 29 bus service, which picks up and drops off within 75 metres of our front door, to ferry us into town and back again each hour between 07:45 and 17:15 from Monday to Saturday. The prospect of being "carless" for the first time in 55 years seemed quite daunting initially but, in view of our current situation and from a common sense aspect, the decision was actually quite straightforward.

The total running costs for the car worked out to about £12 per week, including fuel, and it was only being used for the weekly shopping trip and an occasional appointment elsewhere. A total of about 300 miles per year – other than that, it was standing idle on the drive. We weren't keen on the idea of advertising it and then entertaining prospective buyers at all hours and we were hoping that someone in the family might give it a good home. We decided if that were the case then we wouldn't take any payment, even though the car was valued at around £3,500.

We spoke to Sean, thinking that it might be suitable as a runabout for Sarah or as a first car for Jim but they didn't really have a need for it at that time. We asked Richard and Sam and, as luck would have it, Chris's wife Charlotte was on the lookout for a car. She and Sam came to view it on Friday, July 22nd and, following a test drive around the block, she was really keen. After sorting out her insurance overnight, she collected it the next morning, Saturday, July 23rd. Carole and I were delighted that it was staying in the family and that things had been resolved so quickly, with no fuss. Charlotte took the car to LE Garage Services for its MOT on August 22nd and it passed with no problems, which was a first for her, she said. She then drove to Wales in September and said that it had behaved perfectly.

Carole and I feel that we made the right decision in eliminating one or two more of life's hassles but it will take time to develop a new routine. As for the shopping, Carole seems to favour taking the 29 bus to Tesco, doing the shop as normal and then coming home by taxi, which is what we were doing with the car really. Maybe one day, if she runs out of motivation and/or energy, we may have to think again and try to master the art of online ordering from the Tesco home delivery service. We'll see – early days.

Her Majesty Queen Elizabeth II died on Thursday, September 8th, 2022, whilst taking her traditional summer vacation on the Balmoral Estate in Scotland. For some of us, the Queen has always been there, both in times of celebration and in times of adversity and, regardless of circumstances, she always appeared calm and dignified. Her life has been an extraordinary demonstration of her steadfast commitment to duty. Phillip, her husband of 73 years, had been at her side for almost the entire 70 years of her reign, but his death on April 9th, 2021, brought their physical partnership to an end. I'm sure that must have taken the wind out of her sails and it seemed to have a profound effect on her health. Despite that, she has continued to fulfil the majority of her engagements, even to the point of inviting the newly-selected Liz Truss to Balmoral on September 6th to be appointed officially as Prime Minister. Ordinarily, this audience would take place at Buckingham Palace but the Queen was not due to return to London for another month and this meeting took place only two days before Her Majesty's death. Maybe she sensed that time was of the essence and needed to know that the ship wouldn't be left completely rudderless. Thank you Ma'am, for your compassion and for your wit and wisdom. Your duty is done – may you now rest in peace.

King Charles III has now taken the reins and it remains to be seen how he deals with his new responsibilities. Will he become less outspoken or will he continue to try to influence and urge changes? I know what I am hoping for. His life thus far has proved to be a lengthy apprenticeship and he has spent much of the time rubbing shoulders with everybody who is anybody and countless others who, like me, may be viewed as life's nobodies. He's had the opportunity to master the art of dealing with all kinds from all walks of life and the knowledge which he has gained should now prove invaluable. We all hope that he will succeed in holding his Kingdom together, despite the best efforts of those who may prefer otherwise.

As far as I know, Charlie Boy never golfed, seldom cricketed, hardly soccered but occasionally poloed. If one's exhausted pony should happen to suddenly collapse beneath one in mid-chukka, one faced automatic disrottenqualification and a bugger of a long walk back to the pavilion. His sporting days are behind him and he now faces the ultimate challenge in the fulfilment of his destiny. We wish him well.

CHAPTER 15

Now that I'm running out of things to say, perhaps I'll revert to the customary British tradition of talking about the weather. It is Thursday, August 11th, 2022, and as I write this, we are into day 4 of the second heatwave of the summer and the temperature in this neck of the woods is 31 °C. This is slightly cooler than the 40 °C that was recorded in some places during the first heatwave of July 16th – 19th, but you wouldn't really notice. At Carole's suggestion, I took to soaking a towel in cold water and wearing it like a scarf in order to keep cool and it proved to be very effective. The forecasters tell us that we may see signs of a change by Monday, with rain forecast for a few places and then, hopefully, the oppressive conditions will start to break up.

Speaking of rain, the longest period that I can remember us going without it is about two months, during the summer of 1976. I recall the depressing feeling when we went day after day with no sign of rain, all the while hoping that the next cloud may bring relief. During the morning of Sunday, September 12th, the long-awaited respite finally arrived, coinciding perfectly with the first full day of our holiday at California Sands, Caister. It hardly stopped all that week but we didn't complain because we'd waited so long and we were desperate for the rain, but what irony.

On Monday, November 28th, 2022, Sean attended Sheffield Crown Court at the start of two weeks jury service but, alas, he wasn't allowed to discuss the case. On Thursday, October 6th, 2022, I attended Breaston surgery for my Annual Review with Nurse Suzanne Howarth. The consequences of that escalated into a bit of a saga, the details of which I decided to record as a separate assignment. Carole and I went to Breaston surgery on Saturday morning, October 15th, for covid and flu jabs. It was during that week that we first put out whole monkey nuts for the squirrels in the hope that they might be deterred from dashing across the road to scrump them from No 18. They soon cottoned on to the idea and now turn up on most mornings to collect their ration of four, which they then dash off to bury in various locations around the garden. The ever-vigilant magpies watch this activity from the rooftops and then swoop down to pinch the nuts.

We are now at the end of October and I've not seen any bats or signs of a hedgehog for about a week so I presume they have retired for the winter. The blackbirds and the starlings only come occasionally but Mr Whitestripes turns up on most days, still on his own. Not seen the starling with the club foot for about 5 weeks – maybe the foot has healed and the bird is now indistinguishable from the rest of the gang? The irrepressible squirrels are back to normal, tear-arsing around – maybe they prefer cooler weather? Richard and Sam went down to Mortehoe for a mini-break from December 8th – 11th.

During the early evening of December 31st, 2022, we heard a fox yapping, the first sign that their breeding season was under way - this will usually go on for about 3 to 4 weeks. The yapping fox was heard on most evenings but he seemed to be ploughing a lonely furrow as I can't recall hearing any response to his calls. The vixen's unmistakable reply is a ghastly, blood-curdling scream which might be likened to that of someone being subjected to a gruesome attack. We heard the yapping on most evenings until January 18th, then it wasn't heard again until the 30th, and that was the last time.

For a period of about 3 weeks during February, 2023, a fox visited the patio on most evenings between 19:30 and 20:45 and the more I saw of it, the more I was convinced that it was our estranged Notip. Its size, colouring, the way it moved, the way it looked at me and its general body language and attitude all told me that if it wasn't Notip, it was what the Germans call a "doppleganger". The one thing which prevented a positive ID was the fact that the mark on her right hip, which I had originally thought may be a birthmark, had mysteriously disappeared. Maybe it had been an illusion, maybe it had moulted out, or maybe it was a dead fly on my specs?

Around the middle of February, 2023, a rust-coloured pigeon arrived on the rooftop of one of the houses which back on to our garden. Our daily patio activity had obviously attracted its attention and on the morning of March 4th, it came down to investigate. It sampled the dried mealworms but apparently wasn't impressed because it hasn't been back. Its plumage appeared to be a uniform rust colour from head to tail and devoid of the usual green/purple iridescence around its head and neck and its legs and feet were pink. An unusual-looking bird but it wasn't wearing any ID rings and seemed solitary and quite content to spend the days on its own, making no attempt to mix with the resident flock. That changed at the end of May, however, when a normal-looking grey pigeon arrived on the scene to share the rooftop with Rusty. Within a few days, they were to be seen cavorting and posturing on the ridge tiles, as pigeons do, with the newcomer eventually assuming the dominant position, suggesting to me that Rusty was probably female. At the end of October they both disappeared and I've not seen them since.

On Saturday, April 29th, Long Eaton United beat Stockton Town in the Northern Premier League East Division play-off Final, thereby winning promotion for the second successive season. They will be playing in the Southern League Premier Central Division next season, 2023/24. During April, 2023, our next-door-but-one neighbour Stephen offered to trim the sycamore and our conifers in order to let more light into the garden. No objections from us – feel free. He's been a couple of times but it's not really made much difference – it seems to regenerate while you're looking at it. On April 6th, we spotted hedgehog poo on the patio – the first positive sign that they were active again. I've not been getting up for my midnight snack since November, 2022, when I was ill and I've lost touch with the hogs and the foxes.

On April 12th, Carole called DWP to enquire about Attendance Allowance and she was told that we would be sent a claim form and assessment may then take 12 weeks after receipt of the completed form. The form, which was as thick as a church door, arrived on April 18th, and we spent a fortnight filling it in, returning it on May 5th. The enquiry and the effort proved worthwhile, however, because on June 18th, we were informed that our claim had been approved.

At about 10:00 on Sunday, April 16th, 2022, our mangey fox Tiny Tim turned up, slowly making his way along the front of the houses across the road. I had spotted him and was watching from the window as he arrived at the front door of No 16, where he suddenly came to a halt, turned and stared straight at me, as though he recognised something familiar. As I was beckoning to him to cross over the road, Colin at No 12 chose that moment to come out to his car. That startled Tiny Tim and he did an about-turn, retraced his steps and disappeared down the drive at No 20, from where he had emerged, I suspect. About an hour later he reappeared, slowly making his way down the middle of our back garden – he was really struggling to walk but managed to settle down at the end of the lawn for a rest.

By the time Carole and I sat down for lunch at 11:30, he had disappeared. At about 13:00, Carole went down the garden to fill the bird feeders, only to find Tiny Tim lying dead against the fence under the sycamore. It was almost as if he had come back to the place where he had once found sanctuary – it seemed such a wretched and lonely end to his little life. We read that a fox which is suffering from untreated mange is likely to die within 6 months and, in the case of Tiny Tim, that was just about right. He first came to us in October, 2022, but we hadn't seen him since January 5th – he was the second fox to die in our garden within 7 months and, remarkably, within 3 or 4 metres of where the first one died.

On Thursday, May 11th, 2023, my sister Kathleen rang to tell us that Simon had suffered a heart attack and had been admitted to hospital to have 2 stents fitted. He is now recovering, thankfully, but his experience has been a wake-up call for everyone. Even a puritan lifestyle doesn't guarantee immunity from ill-health and it certainly doesn't need an invitation. On Saturday, May 13th, 2023, Notts County beat Chesterfield in a nail-biting National League play-off final at Wembley. The scores were level after 90 minutes and after extra time but Notts County held their nerve to win the penalty shoot-out 4–3. It would surely have been a gross injustice had Notts County lost this match because Chesterfield finished no less than 25 points behind them in the final League table. This illustrates the nonsense lottery that the play-off system is – sheer torture for all those involved and it's high time that it was scrapped. This also applies to the points-deduction rule in cases of financial irregularities – this punishes the players who have earned the points and the fans who have supported them. Those responsible for these problems walk away unpunished – ludicrously shallow, unjust and unfair.

On Thursday, June 1st, 2023, Carole and I attended Breaston Pharmacy again for our covid booster jabs. Over the following weekend, my NIV machine started to play up – it seemed to be leaking from somewhere, possibly the hose? Sean happened to visit us that weekend and he said that if the NIV needed to be exchanged, he would take it in to the hospital. We called the Royal Derby first thing on Monday (the 5th) and were told that we should take the faulty NIV in, complete with hose and mask, and an exchange machine would be prepared ready for collection. I think they can produce a new SIMcard from my stored calibration data. Sean arrived at 10:30 and was back home with the exchange machine, hose and mask, by 11:40.

On Friday, June 9th, Richard and Sam went down to Mortehoe for a few days, returning on the following Friday, the 16th. Community Nurse Lisa from the Royal Derby rang on Friday, June 9th, to arrange an appointment for a home visit in order to do a blood-gas test. She arrived punctually at 12:00 on Wednesday, June 21st and, following the test and analysis, she said the readings were fine and the results would be passed on to the Team. She couldn't see any reason why anything should be changed but that would be up to the doctors – I didn't hear anything more on that so I presume that everything was satisfactory. It was Long Eaton Carnival on Saturday, June 17th, and the highlight for me was the brief display by a Memorial Flight Hurricane – that sound is unmistakeable.

On July 1st, 2023, I received a message from Alan Ure telling me that there had been changes at Borrowash Vics following the departure of Chairman Frazer Watson and Vice-chairman Ian Anderson. Alan has taken control of the Club as Chairman and a few things need sorting out but he has, however, managed to reach an agreement with Messrs Watson and Anderson regarding a long-term lease on the ground. The Manager and his coaching staff are staying in post for the time being so that should help to steady the ship. It sounds complicated behind the scenes and I'm not exactly sure what, or who, caused this upheaval.

During the month of July, 2023, we had several sightings of a fox in the garden during the daytime and I was pretty sure that it was our estranged Dainty. It seemed that she was not alone, as we also caught the occasional glimpse of what may have been a cub. Dainty's stealthy behaviour and constant glances towards the house suggested that she may indeed have a cub in tow? We hadn't seen her for a year and she seemed lankier but her attitude, general demeanour and ginger coat all suggested that it was

Dainty. She was using the hollow beneath the niger-seed feeders as a den and the Michaelmass daisy patch provided cover from where she could keep watch on the garden. She was here for about a month and August 5th was the last time that we saw her.

On Sunday, July 16th, 2023, grandson Jim boarded a Boeing 787 Dreamliner for the 10-hour, 5,000-mile flight from Manchester to Cancun, Mexico. This was the start of a two-week trip with his School. They spent their first week under canvas amongst the flora, fauna and animal life in the jungle reserve which surrounds the ruined Maya city of Calakmul. The party also spent some time exploring the archaeological site itself. For the second week, they made their way back to civilisation and the east coast town of Akumal, where they took part in activities of a more recreational nature, including scuba diving and snorkelling. After seeing Jim off on his trip on the Sunday, Sean and Sarah departed the following day for a ten-day break in Isla Canela, Spain. They boarded a flight from EM Airport to Faro, Portugal, from where they travelled across the border into Spain by coach for the remaining 30 miles to their hotel. They arrived back on Thursday the 27th, calling in to see us on the way home to Chesterfield to announce their engagement. The wedding date has been set for 11:00 on Saturday, November 25th, 2023, at the Registry Office in Chesterfield. Jim arrived home safely from his trip at lunchtime on Monday, the 31st.

Carole made an appointment to see Dr Smith (new man on the Team) at Breaston surgery on Friday, July 28th, 2023, regarding the cough which she's had for about 3 years. She had also become increasingly concerned about the sore which appeared on the inside of her left shin about 3 months ago. He suspected that the cough may be due to "post-nasal drip" but suggested that she should go for a chest X-ray and blood test in order to eliminate other possible causes. With regard to the sore on her leg, he referred her to the Dermatology Clinic at the Florence Nightingale Community Hospital (formerly DRI) for investigation. In response to his request for a chest X-ray, Long Eaton Health Centre rang on Monday the 31st to offer Carole a 16:20 appointment for the following day, Tuesday, August 1st, which she accepted.

The following Sunday, August 6th, Sean, Sarah and Jim had been to visit us and as they were about to leave for home at 13:30, an ambulance arrived at Stephen's, next door but one. He told us later that his Mum had a fall while the carers were there and they thought that she ought to go to the Queens Med to be checked over. Just as well because they found that she had a couple of broken ribs and she was kept in for 6 weeks. She was then transferred to Ilkeston hospital for a further two weeks before being discharged.

Jim recently started a part-time job serving bar meals at a local pub – it pays well and dealing with the public is always entertaining and should be a useful experience for him. At about 10:00 on the morning of Wednesday, August 9th, a scrawny-looking fox and an equally scrawny-looking cub came to the patio for worms. They were mangey and looked very sad and I thought that mum should be called "Streaky" and the cub "Smoky", as in bacon. They were underweight and seemed to be in a hurry – desperately searching for a square meal, no doubt. Streaky turned up in the afternoon the next day but she spotted me and scurried off. On Saturday, August 12th, our neighbour Stephen came across a hedgehog in his garden – it was struggling to get about and didn't look very well. Only days before, he had found a dead squirrel in the garden, which we thought may well be one of the pair that lived in our garden. The bushy-tailed one is on its own now and still very active but we don't know whether it's male or female so I named it "Scallywag". I think the name is gender neutral and also seems to suit its cheeky face.

Stephen put the hedgehog in a box and called the local rescue centre ("Twiggies") and they came out that same afternoon to collect it. He called them the next day to enquire about the patient and he was told that the hog wasn't well and had been put on antibiotics. We were advised against feeding them on mealworms as they are high in phosphorus content and low in calcium content and may cause bone disease. We now offer dog meat and crushed dog biscuits as an alternative menu and, judging by the empty dishes every morning, this idea is proving popular. We would prefer that it's the hogs and foxes that are enjoying the food and not just a prowling cat but it's not being wasted so we don't really mind. On Tuesday, August 22nd, Stephen got a call from Twiggies to let him know that the sick hedgehog had died. From his description of it, we think it may well have been our old friend Bumbly? Streaky turned up at 08:30 on September 3rd – she is so slight in build, hardly much bigger than a cat and such a pathetic sight.

On Friday, August 18th, 2023, Carole visited the Dermatology Clinic regarding the sore on her leg. No fewer than 6 white coats had a jolly good look at it and the consensus of opinion was that it should be removed. She would be notified within three weeks re an appointment for the procedure. In fact, they called on Tuesday, August 29th, to offer her an appointment at 15:45 the next day, which she accepted. She turned up expecting to have the sore removed but they decided to do a preliminary biopsy to determine whether removal was actually necessary. Because the sore was close to the shin bone, there wouldn't be much flesh to stitch in order to close the wound, which they thought could be quite large. Smacks of too many cooks putting the cart before the horse. The biopsy wound needed two stitches and she was advised to make an appointment at her local surgery in two weeks to have those removed, by which time the result of the biopsy should be known.

On August 21st, 2023, the news came from Richard that Hannah and her new partner Carl are expecting their first baby on February 18th, 2024. Carole attended Breaston surgery on Thursday, August 24th, for a blood test in connection with her cough. On Monday, September 4th, 2023, she attended the Queens Med for her annual glaucoma check and the pressure readings were the same as last year, which was good news. She had a telephone appointment with Dr Smith on Saturday, September 9th and we were relieved to be told that her chest X-ray was clear. He would, however, like her to take another blood test as the liver function reading indicates Vitamin D deficiency and he wants to double-check. Meanwhile, he prescribed a nasal spray which hopefully may solve the cough problem but this sometimes takes a while to become effective.

On Thursday the 14th, she had an appointment with Nurse Ali at Breaston to have the stitches removed from her leg – no news about the biopsy. Whilst there, she made joint appointments for us on Friday, October 6th at 16:10 (flu jabs and covid boosters) and also on Thursday, October 12th at 09:50 for her repeat blood test for Dr Smith and my routine blood test for my annual review on November 1st, 2023. Carole had another traipse to the Florence Nightingale on September 27th, just to be told that the biopsy revealed that the sore is not cancerous but they would like to see her again in three months.

Sunday, September 17th, 2023, was Carole's birthday and Sean, Sarah and Jim came with McDonalds' breakfast. Following weeks of pondering, I made the decision to join Facebook (FB) and so Sean set up an account for me in the Borrowash, Spondon, Ockbrook & Chaddesden group (BOS&CH). I submitted my first post the next day on the subject of GIC cricket and that was approved by Admin Pete Barnett within hours. It would appear that they are prepared to accept my Posts but a FB rule says that I'm not allowed to reply to comments on my post or make general comments until I have held an account for a month. It would also appear that I may send private messages via "Messenger" if the recipient is a "friend" and I may send messages to others if I "tag" them, i.e. name them but I don't know how to do that?

I was pleased with the response to my first post but the restriction on replies was a bit frustrating. Sean proposed me as a member of FB legsreunited and that was approved on September 24th. I broke the ice with that group by telling them who I was and when I was at LEGS and was pleasantly surprised that some folks actually remembered me. I submitted a second post on the BSO&CH group on the topic of Borrowash Youth Club (1959/60) and a third post on Borrowash Youth Club cricket team (1950 to 1956) and also Mrs Tunnicliffe using our Kimberley Road meadow. Only limited response to Borrowash YC 1959/60, no response on the YC cricket team and hardly any to Mrs Tunnicliffe's time at Borrowash.

Bunter at No 16 set off in Dave's Fiesta (she had previously told Carole that it belonged to her) before 07:00 on Thursday, September 28th, as though she was going to work, though her normal workdays are Mondays, Wednesdays and Saturdays. She didn't come home in the car and it was missing until 09:30 the following Monday morning when the long-absent Dave turned up in it. This was the first time he'd been seen since he disappeared in July last year but he is now visiting regularly. He arrives at about 09:30 on Tuesdays, Thursdays and Fridays, after Bunter has taken the lads to school, and leaves at 14:30 before they come home.

It seems fairly obvious that he doesn't have a job to go to. He doesn't visit at weekends or on the days that Bunter goes to work when her parents are here childminding. It would seem that the part-time, "happy families" relationship they have doesn't involve their kids, which seems an odd way for two married adults to behave. I wonder how Bunter explained Dave's absence to the kids and also the fact that the Fiesta had recently disappeared when they'd got used to seeing it stuck in the road virtually unattended for fourteen months. I suspect that my suspicions about Dave's absence are becoming more plausible with each passing day.

On Tuesday, October 3rd, Donkey Dick (DD) and Blobby at No 18 were seen to be packing his car to the rafters with all their worldly belongings – could it be that they were moving out? DD had been living there since Blobby's brother moved out in September, 2019, perhaps to university but he'd hardly moved out when DD moved in. The result of the liaison between DD and Blobby was born in June, 2019, presumably conceived, therefore, in September, 2018, when she was barely sixteen? DD has to rank as the most unsociable, antisocial, irritating, arrogant tosser that I have ever set eyes on and he has an uncontrollable compulsion to prance about on the front row at every opportunity. We think that he worked the twilight shift at Aldi on a zero-hours contract – on the odd evenings when he went to work, he would leave at 17:15, returning home between 01:00 and 02:00. His car was fitted with an alarm which seemed to have a mind of its own and would be triggered for no apparent reason at any hour of the day or night, usually within minutes of him parking up.

He spent his leisure time, which was most days, all day, either in bed or taxying Blobby the two-mile round trip to work and back on the two days per week that she bothered to go, depositing and collecting the kid from playschool en route. When he wasn't on taxi duty, he was obsessed with cleaning his car 4 times a week, inside with the hoover and outside with the customary hosepipe. This was despite repeated appeals from Severn Trent for consumers to refrain from using hosepipes and sprinklers when cleaning cars and/or watering gardens. Not being the householder, he was probably the only one in the street who wasn't paying water rates. It's all a matter of awareness and consideration for others. Que?

During the month of October we frequently saw foxes wandering around the garden during the daytime – Streaky and Smoky (neither of whom looked very well), Dainty, Notip (?) and one or two others who we didn't recognise. We were also treated to what had become a rare sight in the garden over the last 5 years, or so – coloured butterflies. These were of the red admiral variety and as many as 6 or 8 at a time were feeding on the nectar provided by the flowers of the ivy which was smothering Kevin's garage. Carole and I had appointments at Breaston at 16:00 on Friday, October 6th, for our flu jabs and covid boosters. Richard and Sam came home on that same day after spending the week in Mortehoe.

On Monday, October 9th, I received a letter from the newly-appointed Practice Manager at Moores Dental Surgery – Sarah Smith had obviously moved on and been replaced by Josine van den Berg. From the content of the letter, I gathered that nothing had changed and there were no guarantees in the event that I should require treatment for any reason. It was no more than a circular really and, in the circumstances, I didn't think it warranted a reply. FB Admin Pete Barnett called me at 11:00 on Wednesday, October 11th, for a chat – I'm not sure why other than maybe he just had some time to kill.

On that same afternoon, Carole had an appointment at Breaston for her annual asthma review with Nurse Suzanne. Suzanne asked about the nasal spray which Dr Smith had prescribed and Carole said that she hadn't noticed any improvement. Suzanne prescribed a tablet to be taken in conjunction with the spray and would like to see her again in 4 weeks – she has an appointment at 14:30 on Wednesday, November 22nd. We were due to have our blood tests at 09:50 on October 12th but the surgery called just after 08:00 on the morning to tell us that Nurse Lynne had tested positive for covid. The appointments were rearranged for 08:20 on November 9th, 2023, and my Annual Review was rearranged for 09:50 on November 16th, 2023.

During the month of September, our neighbour Kevin filled two small skips with debris, some of which we think may have been from his kitchen ceiling. It seems that water had been leaking from somewhere and it had eventually seeped through the outer brickwork between the toilet window and the back door. The kitchen ceiling had become sufficiently waterlogged so as to cause it to partially collapse, or so we were told. The leak was eventually repaired and the wall and door dried out and the fungi which had sprouted from the damp brickwork disappeared. A team of three from Maple Tree Care arrived at 08:30 on Monday, October 16th, to clear the bramble which had turned his back garden into an impenetrable jungle and was now also beginning to emerge in the front garden. An avenue was cut through the middle of the bramble for the entire length of the garden, using a remotely-controlled "mole". This enabled access so that the remainder of the bramble over the whole area could be cleared and the debris shredded in an operation which took all day.

The team returned the following day, Tuesday, and the "climber" spent 5 hours removing the towering 50-foot sycamore and a 40-foot silver birch, bough by bough. They were back again on Wednesday to rotovate the back garden and also to cut down the 15-foot buddleia which was smothering the telegraph pole at the front. Whilst this work was essential, the consequences are that not only have we lost the visiting red admirals but also our thriving sparrow colony. Maybe the birds will return if things ever quieten down? We are led to believe that new doors, windows and soffits are included in Kevin's plans so it's beginning to look like a lengthy operation. On Monday, November 20th, 2023, some workmen arrived, seemingly to repair or replace the damaged kitchen, or so we thought. Quite a lot of articles of all descriptions have been removed and deposited in several large skips and it is now looks like a house-clearance operation. Kevin has moved out for the duration but, hopefully, he will be back to resume normal service.

I had been making enquiries regarding an excellent photo which features six of the "down brook gang" posing on the bridge over the brook at Borrowash. Dickie Litchfield, John Church and Doug Smith are all in the photo but when I contacted them, none could remember who the photographer was. This was in spite of the fact that the Brownie box camera which was used to take it actually belonged to Dickie! I chatted with Doug for about 20 minutes on the morning of October 17th, and he could remember the photo being taken but not the photographer. He said he was pleased to hear from me and told me that he still had a problem with his throat, despite having two operations since we last met. On

October 19th, I decided to post the photo, together with an appeal for info, on FB and though the response was good, the mystery remains unsolved. It was my 77th birthday that same day (another milestone safely passed) and Richard and Sam came to see us for an hour in the afternoon. Sean, Sarah and Jim came with McDonalds and my ration of cheese biccies on Sunday morning, the 22nd. On the afternoon of the 25th, Carole went into Nottingham to meet Grace for a catch-up.

The following day, Monday, October 23rd, 2023, I received a message from Mike Ronan to say that his book was ready and did I want to meet up, or should he mail it, or should he deliver it? I chose the latter option and we decided that Thursday morning, October 26th, was suitable and he would ring me before he left home to check on directions. He arrived at 10:40 on Thursday morning carrying my signed copy of his autobiography "There is only one Mike Ronan". This was our first meeting in 30 years but, sadly, he couldn't stay long because Margaret had gone out without a key and she might be worrying if there was nobody in when she got home. His hip surgery was eventually carried out at the beginning of September. It was done under local anaesthetic and he could hear the surgeon and his team talking as they were working. He hasn't felt any pain at all and was already walking unaided and driving and appeared to be making excellent progress. Because our meeting was brief he said he would like to come and see us again when we've had time to read the book and he'll answer any queries we may have.

On Sunday, October 29th, Sean, Sarah and Jim went up to Edinburgh for a 3-day break, returning at teatime on Wednesday, November 1st. They visited the city a few weeks ago when Jim was checking out his University options and they were so impressed with what they saw that they decided to return for another look. Carole recently saw a hedgehog when putting out the food at around 21:00 GMT. It's interesting that, having put the clocks back 1 hour last Sunday, the hedgehog arrived at 20:00 BST on the Monday evening! This seems to suggest that their night-time activity is triggered by the fading light and not by an alarm clock. Great-granny Kathleen called on Monday, October 30th with news of an addition to the family – Simon's daughter Phoebe (Cooper) had given birth to a boy, Finlay Harold.

On the morning of Wednesday, November 1st, Carole arrived home from the weekly shopping trip and as she was carrying the bags from the taxi, she went all her length on the driveway. Fortunately, the bags cushioned the impact to some extent but she suffered bruising around her mouth, nose and eyes. This was probably caused by the impact on her specs which, fortunately, didn't shatter or her injuries might have been far more serious. On Friday, November 3rd, she went to Nottingham, black eyes and all, to meet Kevin and Charlotte Stansall. On the afternoon of Wednesday, November 8th, she was back in Nottingham to meet Caroline. On Friday, November 3rd, Sean went to Butlins, Skegness, with two work colleagues, Gary, Leo and Stephen for a weekend of "stag" celebrations. He got home in one piece on the Monday after having a really good time – plenty of booze and laughs but not much sleep.

We went to Breaston surgery at 08:30 on Thursday, November 9th, for our rearranged blood tests, with Sam once again providing the transport. Sean, Sarah and Jim came with McDonalds' breakfast on Saturday the 11th – only two weeks to go till their big day. On Sunday the 12th, Richard and Sam went down to London to see Abba the Voyage, travelling from Derby by coach and arriving at their hotel in London by early afternoon. They were taken by coach from their hotel to the Abba Arena for the evening performance and then back to their hotel afterwards. Following an overnight stay and breakfast, they had time for some sightseeing before the return journey to Derby on Monday evening. I submitted another post to FB, this time about my golfing outings with Ron Newton and Ken Porter – good response again.

At 09:50 on Thursday, November 16th, 2023, we were once again at Breaston surgery, this time for my Annual Review with Nurse Suzanne. The blood results were fine but the uric acid level could be further reduced simply by increasing the Allopurinol dosage. Changes to medication must now be authorised by the newly-appointed Practice Pharmacist so we made appointments for December 5th, first with Nurse Naomi Gill at 09:50 for a blood test and then with Pharmacist Kashmira Patel at 10:10. Suzanne said that I would need to bring a urine sample when I come for my blood test. After discussing my medication with Kashmira, she proposed that we increase the Allopurinol dose from

100mg to 200mg daily, i.e. two tablets each day instead of one. My vitals on the day are recorded under "Annual Review" and "My Vitals".

On Friday, November 17th, Sarah called to see us after visiting her Dad in Draycott. Her forthcoming marriage to Sean had inspired her to write a heartfelt poem for the occasion and she wanted to give us a private recitation. The following day, a group of their friends went bowling as part of the build-up to next weekend. Rusty Pigeon went missing during the weekend of October 28th – still no sign of her or her mate and no sign of the hedgehogs since then either – probably taken to their beds till the spring? Workmen turned up at Kevin's on Monday the 20th and spent the week clearing stuff out of the house and also removing the garage roof. We've not seen Kevin since that day and we think he's moved out until the renovation is finished. On Friday the 24th, Carole went to Breaston surgery to see Dr Smith again – he has prescribed a different nasal spray and asked her to take another blood test. Her appointment for that is at 10:20 on Thursday, January 4th, 2024.

The Wedding - Saturday, November 25th, 2023. The big day finally arrived, not only for Sean and Sarah, but for everyone who knows them. The planning went well and anything that's not done now will have to stay undone! The ceremony took place in the registry office at Chesterfield Town Hall and those present were Jim, Richard and Sam and the bride's friend Dr Sarah and her partner Tom. Official witnesses were Dr Sarah, Jim and Richard. Following the ceremony, the seven of them made their way to the Ringwood Hall Hotel and Spa where they spent the rest of the day relaxing. Dinner in the evening was followed eventually by an overnight stay and breakfast – and a good time was had by all.

Sean, Sarah and Jim came to see us the day after the wedding sporting their wedding attire. After spending an hour with us, Carole and the three of them departed for Draycott to lunch with Sarah's Dad Adrian and Stepmum Megan. Following a comparatively restful day on Monday, Sean and Sarah travelled to Disneyland, Paris on Tuesday for a three day mini-break.

ADDENDA

Between December, 2018 and May, 2021, when I was either ill, or recovering from being ill, I didn't keep a diary because I didn't really have the inclination or the energy. In the big picture, it was not a priority and it was easy to get out of the habit. My notebook scribblings weren't always dated and so, in terms of reliable and positive memory-joggers, I didn't have a lot to fall back on for that period. I'm not sure whether it's a bonus or a handicap but I seem to have been blessed with a memory which retains the kind of rubbish that no one is remotely interested in.

I have devoted quite a lot of the text to my two most recent visits to hospital and the effect that those experiences and the covid restrictions have had on our lives. By choice, I spent my daytime waking hours at my workplace (the dining table), composing my drivel and watching the garden wildlife, from squirrels, bats and birds to buttercups, evening primroses and snapdragons. My night-time waking hours, usually from midnight till about 01:30, I spent with a mug of tea and a sudoku whilst keeping one eye on the patio for visitors before going back to bed to finish my night's sleep. This gave me the opportunity to appreciate some of the nocturnal activity in the garden, particularly the hedgehogs and the foxes. The luxury of being able to go back to bed was a sort of recompense for all the mornings when my 03:00 alarm used to let me know that it was time to get up and get out on the milkround. If I learnt anything at all, it was that there is a lot more to these animals than most of us realise.

My routine changed, however, in November, 2022, when I succumbed to a chest infection and was confined to the bedroom for about 10 days. Since then, negotiating the stairs has become a once-a-day challenge – down in the morning and back up at bedtime. In order to make this possible, Carole brings me breakfast (poached egg on toast) at around 05:00 each morning, after which I get myself washed and dressed before making my way downstairs for the day. All this means, of course, that I've lost touch with "our friends in the night" and can no longer be sure who visits us and who doesn't.

The Wedding seemed to be a convenient place at which to draw a line under Memory Lane, at least for now. Despite all the things that I've included, I don't doubt that there are many more which have temporarily slipped through the net. It's a fair bet that some of these would come back to me in odds and sods and I'd then have the job of inserting them into their appropriate place. The outcome of the on-going issues such as medical appointments and Kevin's renovation project will no doubt be revealed at some stage in the future. There has to be a cut-off point somewhere otherwise the assignment would just be "work in progress" and never be finished. I am not so pretentious as to label Memory Lane "memoirs" or "autobiography" because that type of publication is usually attributed to folks who distinguish themselves in some way during their lifetime. They then sit down and write about it in the hope that folks will then cough up for the privilege of reading about it.

When I started this assignment in August, 2017, it was intended to be a brief essay about the memories I have of my Nana, an idea which was inspired by Hetty's death in July, 2017, and Richard's reaction to it. Once I had begun to write, all sorts of memories came flooding back and I just let the keyboard have its wicked way with me. Things developed to such a degree that it may now serve as a response to the suggestion that Richard and Sean put to me some while ago that I should write about my life, a challenge which I rejected at the time. It was never meant to be anything other than a journal or a list of my memories, some of which may not be totally reliable. I have tried to keep events in chronological order and the people involved in them "in line abreast" so that we all cross the finishing line together. This may make for disjointed reading due to my inexperienced, scatterbrained, sausage-fingered clumsiness.

My biggest regret is that I wasn't inquisitive enough when I was a youngster and I'm constantly searching for answers and explanations to things which still puzzle me. The problem is that most of the folks with all the answers are no longer here to ask and the moral of the story is that if you're not sure, don't be afraid to ask. My efforts on these pages are a tribute to Grandmas and Grandpas everywhere. Without them, none of the folks mentioned above would ever have been around to help create my memories, I wouldn't be here to write about them and you wouldn't be here to read about them.

OBITUARIES

ALAN HUNT died on February 20th, 2019. A long-time friend and godfather to my son Sean. A real gent.

GEOFF PADGETT died on November 25th, 2022, aged about 73. A well-liked young man, he joined the army at 18 and served in Northern Ireland, where he chose to get married and settle down.

ROD GROUNSELL died on November 9th, 2022, aged 77. Rod was a member of the "Down Brook Gang" when we were teenagers and I remember him as the most amiable of people who always had a smile on his face.

NEV HARDY died in August, 2022, aged 93. He gave me so much support and encouragement when I was playing football with the Vics and darts for the Exservicemens' Club. Another one that I never caught up with before it was too late. Extremely sad news.

JOHN DILLEY died in January, 2019. He was, by nature, a quietly-spoken and modest man but beneath the amiable exterior lay a tough competitor who stood no nonsense.

ROGER TATTERSALL, former assistant pro to Mike Ronan at the Erewash Valley GC, had been suffering from cancer, I believe, and died in October, 2021, aged 68. He retired from his professional career at the age of 58 due to ill-health. He had travelled extensively after the days when I knew him at Erewash, his first move being to nearby Coxmoor GC and subsequently as far afield as New Zealand before eventually returning to work in the UK. When I first met him, Roger was about 6 feet tall and 15 stones and he poured every ounce of his substantial frame into the back of a golf ball. I've never seen anyone hit a ball harder or further – you could almost hear it wheeze! He was also a talented cricketer, I believe.

I read in the Derby Telegraph obituaries that former Cheltenham travelling companion MICK DARBY had died in 2021. I lost touch with him and Barry Clark when I left Rolls Royce in 1978.

The ever-flamboyant TONY BEARDSLEY died on February 29th, 2016, aged 72. Typically, the Big Fella simply had to choose the last day of February in a leap year on which to make his final exit! He was born to be the leader of the pack and that is probably how he is remembered by those who knew him.

The always-obliging and popular TONY NEWTON died on May 13th, 2016, aged 71. Known endearingly to us all as "Newt", this man had an impish sense of humour and a heart of gold and would do anything to help anybody.

Whilst browsing Facebook, I happened to stumble on the announcement of the death of JOHN GREGORY. I first met John when we started at Long Eaton Grammar School together in September, 1958. After leaving school, we went through Rolls Royce Apprentice Training School and also Derby Technical College together. He was also godfather to my eldest son Richard. He left RR soon after completing his apprenticeship in order to concentrate on building what was to become a successful telecommunications business. He was ambitious and street-wise and was always destined to succeed. He died on October 21st, 2021, from the effects of dementia, which seems strangely out of character for the confident and positive John that we remember. By strange coincidence, my Dad and his father Claude were classmates at Risley School in the 1920s.

ALAN ROTHWELL, former teacher of German and Latin at LEGS, died on February 12th, 2018, aged about 86, I believe. This man was a breath of fresh air compared to the largely stuffy folks who were on the Staff during my time at the School. He insisted on calling us all by our Christian names, which was hitherto unheard of. After leaving LEGS in 1963, he went to work in Canada, where he gained his Masters' Degree in German, and then in London before returning to his roots near Pontefract. He joined the Staff at Ackworth School in 1966 and became Head of German and Housemaster until his retirement in 1994. Being part of his German classes is one of the happier memories of my schooldays. It was a real treat to meet up with him again after 40 years when we both attended a LEGS reunion in 2002.

Printed in Great Britain
by Amazon